My Child: 2 to 5 years

This book has been published by the HSE (2019). This is the sixth edition (December 2020). You will be given a copy by your public health nurse close to your child's second birthday.

'My Child: 2 to 5 years' is filled with expert advice from health professionals in the HSE. These include doctors, nurses, psychologists, parenting experts, dietitians and many more. Our team has worked to give you the best advice on caring for your child. We hope that you can use this book, and our mychild.ie website, as a companion for every step of your child's first 5 years.

For more information on child health, visit mychild.ie

This is the fifth edition. It was first published in 2005 and last reviewed in 2019.

GW00566293

© Health Service Executive 2019

First published: 2005 (version 1.0)
Reviewed: 2009 (version 2.0)
Updated: 2015, 2019, 2020 (version 5.0 in April and version 6.0 in December)
ISBN: 978-1-78602-112-0

This December 2020 (version 6.0) edition has updated information on:

- feeding your child (pages 16 to 22)
- sleeping (pages 29 to 33)
- chickenpox – treatment (page 55)

Updates are made to individual sections when we become aware of changes to health guidelines or advice. Reviews take place every few years when the entire book is reviewed by experts.

Your public health nurse: _____

Your health centre: _____

Contents

ISBN: 978-1-78602-112-0

The information in this book, including the resources and links, does not replace medical advice from healthcare professionals such as your public health nurse or GP. Everyone is different. Always consult a healthcare professional to give you the medical advice and care you need. All efforts have been made to make sure that this book reflects the most up-to-date medical advice at the time of publication. Developments in healthcare are happening all the time, including new information on a range of issues. We will make every effort to incorporate new information into the text for the next reprint of this book.

Photos unless otherwise stated are stock images and have been posed by models.

Welcome to My Child: 2 to 5 years

This book has lots of information to help you care for yourself and your child over the next three years. It is part of a series of books and a website called mychild.ie from the HSE.

We asked parents what information would help them most during their child's early years.

Parents told us that they want:

- common-sense information and tips on the general care of their child
- information about their child's development
- advice about what to do if their child has a problem
- details of what people and services to get in touch with for help and support

They also told us they wanted this information to be available online and in a printed version to keep at home.

My Child is based on the most up-to-date information available within the health service, and on the experience and knowledge of child health and support services, voluntary organisations and parent groups.

Each child is special and unique. Whether you are a new parent, or you have done this before, we want to help you every step of the way.

As your child grows, their personality is developing alongside their physical development. With your support, your child can grow to be to be a healthy, resilient and confident person. All of the information in this book and in the two previous books in this series is online at mychild.ie. Sincere thanks to all who helped to create these books, especially the parents.

> This book is the last in a set of three books for parents:
>
> - My Pregnancy
> - My Child: 0 to 2 years
> - My Child: 2 to 5 years

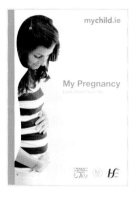

Health checks for your child

Your child will usually have four planned appointments for healthcare checks between the ages of 2 and 5. These are free of charge.

Did you know?

Every child under the age of 6 can get a GP visit card. This means you can take your child to visit their GP for free. It also covers care for children with asthma up to the age of 6. Go to hse.ie and search for 'under 6s GP visit card'.

You will get reminders about your child's next check. If you have changed your address, please tell your local health centre.

When	What happens at the health check
Usually between 3 and 4 years	This check will take place at your local health centre or in your own home. Your public health nurse: • weighs your child and measures their height • checks that your child is developing as expected • checks your child's hearing and eyes • discusses your child's and family's health, nutrition and safety • talks to you about any concerns you may have about your child
4 to 5 years	This check takes place in school when your child is in junior infants. You will be asked to sign a consent form before it takes place. The form has questions about your child's general health. Your school public health nurse or your local public health nurse will read your signed form before the check. They will check your child's hearing and eyes. If you or the nurse are concerned about any part of the health check, your child may be sent for a further check. Sometimes they will be referred to a specialist.

Taking care of yourself as a parent

Being a parent is one of the most important jobs. It is also the job where hardly anybody gets any training. What matters most to your child is that you are there to love, support, guide and care for them.

It is important to realise that no parent is perfect. Everybody makes mistakes. Every parent finds some parts of parenting difficult. You are already juggling many roles in your daily life and doing the best you can for your child, your family and yourself.

Tips for parents

Being a parent can be one of the hardest jobs you have ever done! But it can also be the most rewarding. Making small changes can help you manage the challenges of being a parent.

Be kind to yourself

These years will pass quickly, so enjoy your time with your child. Focus attention on what is important.

Be kind to yourself. Talk to yourself as if you were talking to a friend. What would you tell them?

Look at it from your child's point of view

It can be very stressful when your child is having a meltdown. Remember this is their way of showing their emotions. It can help if you try to see their point of view.

Always be clear with your child about what you expect of them. For example, imagine you have brought your child to a toy shop. They want everything and have a meltdown. To prevent this from happening, it is best to prepare them for the trip. Tell them beforehand: "We are going to the toy shop and you can pick one thing."

Take a break

All parents need some free time and some fun away from their children. Looking after your needs helps you to look after the needs of your family too. Ask your partner or family member to look after your child while you take a rest or go out.

Draw a line under it

All parents have good days and bad days. The bad days can be hard. You may find you have thoughts like: "Is this behaviour going to last all day?"

A simple change in mind-set can turn the day around. Try saying something like: "Let's start fresh after lunch. This morning was tricky. We are putting this behind us."

Little ears are listening

Be careful about how you speak about your child in front of them as little ears are always listening. Children will live up to both high and low expectations. If you talk about your children always ignoring you and always fighting, they're more likely to keep doing just that.

Acknowledge when things go wrong

It's ok to say: "I'm having a bad day. I'm sorry that I shouted at you. I love you and let's go for a walk." This is setting a good example for your child and also acknowledging that parents are human too.

Pick your battles

It is important not to try and change everything. Small changes can make a big difference. You should celebrate the small wins. See makeastart.ie for advice on making healthier changes for your child.

Give your child a choice. For example, asking them if they want to wear red or blue socks may stop them saying: "I am not going to wear any socks." Praise them if they make a choice.

You may choose to sometimes ignore small misbehaviours if your child is not hurting themselves or anyone else. Ignoring these behaviours will often make them stop.

Let your child make small mistakes and learn from them

Encourage your child's independence by allowing them do things for themselves. Give them the space to safely make small mistakes and learn from them.

Instead of saying: "If you jump in that puddle your feet will get wet," let them do it. They will learn from the experience.

Tune into your child

Every child is different. Some children are quiet and will love playing with puzzles and jigsaws, while others have high energy levels and need to run around a lot.

Tune into what your child likes and figure out what makes them happy. Have fun together doing activities or games that suit their personality.

No such thing as a perfect family

Sometimes it can be good to have a reality check when you've been looking at social media. Most people portray the best versions of themselves and their families on social media. Often that perfect family photo required several takes and sometimes a filter.

Most people don't photograph the tantrums or poo explosion. Give yourself a break from social media. The perfect family does not exist.

Show them how to solve problems

Children are always learning from how we cope with problems or mistakes along the way. Depending on their age, you can begin to teach them problem-solving skills early. Praise them for solving smaller problems themselves.

If you feel that one bad day has merged into a bad week or month, it might help to talk to your public health nurse or GP. They can guide you to services that can support you.

Families come in all shapes and sizes

No matter what your family structure is, children do well when they are loved and cared for in a safe and supportive environment. What matters to children is how they are parented and supported as they grow and develop.

All parents face challenges. But some parents may face additional challenges due to their family structure. Talk to your child and explain that families come in different shapes and sizes.

Parenting as a couple

As you adjust to family life, your relationship with your partner may change. Your relationship might grow stronger as you get to know your child together. Occasionally tension can arise, especially when one or both of you feel tired and stressed. You may find you have different opinions about certain aspects of parenting.

Take care of your relationship. It might help if you:

✔ make time for each other – try and do things as a couple

✔ talk openly together and calmly share your feelings

✔ listen to each other

✔ share the household chores

✔ allow your partner to develop their own style of parenting

✔ try not to argue in front of your child

✔ try to have individual time with your child – this will strengthen your bond with your child while giving your partner a break

Same-sex couples face the same challenges as all other parents but might also have to deal with additional ones such as discrimination or lack of understanding. Talk to your child and explain that families come in different shapes and sizes.

It is illegal to discriminate against someone because of their gender, family status, sexual orientation and other grounds. See citizensinformation.ie and ihrec.ie

Shared parenting for parents who live apart

Parents play a very important role in their child's life, no matter what kind of relationship they have with each other. Shared parenting lets your child build a positive and loving relationship with both parents.

Tips for shared parenting include:

Keep in touch

Encourage your child to be in contact with their other parent. Keep in contact with the other parent through phone calls or online. Send them copies of your child's preschool news or school reports so they are aware of the progress your child is making. This shows your child that both their parents love and care for them.

Let the other parent know about preschool or school plays, parent and teacher meetings or other events that parents are expected to attend – it is important for your child that both parents attend if possible.

Make both homes feel special

Your child needs to feel at home in both parents' homes. They need both families to love and accept them.

Simple things can help. Let your child have a place for their own toothbrush, a special blanket and toys. This is a sign that they belong and are not merely passing through.

Parent together

Sometimes you may have a difficult relationship with the other parent. Try not to let this affect your child's relationship with them.

As far as possible, both parents should try to agree and to stick with the same rules and strategies for parenting.

Parenting alone

Sometimes it's not possible to share the parenting duties for your child. There are over 200,000 one-parent families in Ireland today. Children do well when they are loved and cared for in a safe and supportive environment.

If you are parenting alone, you may feel you aren't able to fill all the roles you need to. It is useful to focus on your strengths and skills — on what you can do rather than what you can't.

✔ Take time to adjust and adapt to your role as a lone parent – remember that we all learn on the job when it comes to parenting.

✔ Focus on your strengths and skills.

✔ It is not easy to be a parent so have realistic expectations of yourself.

✔ Be kind to yourself – you have a lot to organise and a lot of responsibility.

✔ Make sure you make some time for yourself and the things you like to do.

✔ We all need help and support – don't be afraid to ask for help and support from family and friends.

Parenting after the death of your partner

The death of your partner is a very difficult and emotional time for you and your family. If you are in this situation, you may feel unable to cope. You may feel uncertain about the future that you had planned together.

It is important to talk to friends and family for support. Do not be afraid to ask for professional help and advice. You might need help coping with finances and supporting your child or children.

Help your child to understand what has happened by explaining it to them in a way that is appropriate for their age. Talk to your GP. They can provide you with information on local bereavement support services. They can also help you to work through some of the difficult emotions you may be experiencing at this time. Search 'bereavement' on citizensinformation.ie for advice if you have been bereaved.

Older parents

Many parents are having children later in life for many reasons. There are both benefits and challenges to having children at any age. At an older age you may have more financial stability and support than you would have had in your 20s and 30s.

Despite this, you face the same challenges as any parent. You may have extra challenges. Your own parents might be elderly or unwell or you may have teenage children.

All parents struggle with energy levels, especially when children are younger and sleep is an issue. All parents need help and support at different times. It is good to talk to parents with children of similar ages as your child. You will be able to share common experiences and challenges and get support, advice and friendship.

Younger parents

As a younger parent you face similar challenges to any other parent. There may be additional challenges. You might worry about balancing family life with education and finding work.

On the other hand, younger parents probably have more energy to deal with the demands of a young child.

- Consider staying with your parents if they are supporting you.
- There may also be local community supports for parents. Your public health nurse will have information on these.
- Speak to other parents and parents the same age as you if possible. Get support and information from them.
- Like any parent, you will need to take a break and spend time with your friends. Ask your family and friends for help.
- If you are in school or college, talk to a teacher you trust. This will help them to understand that you have other priorities as well as your education.
- Talking to your partner, family member or trusted friend can help you deal with the ups and downs of being a parent.

For couples who are separating or divorcing

Separation or divorce can be stressful for a family. It is normal for you and your child to be upset. You will need to balance dealing with your own emotions and looking after the needs of your child.

Caring for yourself during a separation or divorce

- Get support and help from others, such as family and friends.
- Look after yourself. Eat, sleep, rest, take exercise and reduce the amount of alcohol you drink.
- Keep telling yourself that this upsetting time will pass.
- Be positive about your future. Make realistic plans for yourself and your child or children.
- Contact organisations such as Tusla (the Child and Family Agency), which offers family mediation and counselling services. These services can help to ease your stress and fears and have a positive impact on your child. See tusla.ie

Helping your child through a separation or divorce

- ✔ Love, support and reassure your child.
- ✔ Explain why you are separating or divorcing. Reassure your child that it is because of difficulties in your relationship as a couple and it is not their fault.
- ✔ Both parents need to give the same explanation in a way that is suitable for your child's age.
- ✔ Talk to other adults who are involved in caring for your child, such as their teacher. It is important that they are made aware of any big changes in your child's home life.
- ✔ Listen to your child's feelings and the reasons they are angry or sad. Sit down with them so it is easy to make eye contact. Eye contact lets them know that you are listening to them.
- ✔ Try to spend individual time with each child. Simply spending time with your child can encourage them to talk.
- ✔ Encourage your child to spend time with their friends doing normal things like playing.

What to say:

- Tell your child that they can still love both parents. They don't have to take sides.
- Tell your child that it's ok to talk about their feelings, worries or anger.
- Respect your child – tell them about the process of separating from your partner and involve them in decisions as much as you can.
- Do not speak badly about your partner and why you are separating, no matter how you may feel. Your child may feel guilty about loving their other parent while they try to be loyal to you.

If you or your child find it hard to cope with a separation or divorce, there are professionals who can help.

There is a range of support services available:

- Citizens Information Centre: 0761 07 4000 and citizensinformation.ie
- COSC (The National Office for the Prevention of Domestic, Sexual and Gender-based Violence): whatwouldyoudo.ie
- Money Advice and Budgeting Service (MABS): 0761 07 2000 and mabs.ie
- Barnardos: 01 453 0355
- Your GP
- Your public health nurse
- Social work services from tusla.ie

Getting extra support

There may be times when you need extra support from professionals to help your child and your family.

You are not alone in looking for help. Other parents need extra support at times too.

Getting extra support when needed is a smart thing to do. It shows that you value your family.

Reliable information, access to appropriate childcare and parenting programmes can help you as a parent.

Parenting courses

Many parents attend parenting programmes. A positive parenting programme can give you tips on how to:

- develop positive relationships
- improve communication between you and your child
- help build your child's confidence and independence
- encourage resilience and problem-solving skills in your child
- manage misbehaviour
- develop your own skills and confidence in raising your family
- create a safe and nurturing environment
- develop positive routines
- teach your child new skills and behaviours

Parenting courses are a great opportunity to meet other parents and share experiences.

Generally, parenting programmes are age-specific and they may also be about a particular topic. They can be delivered through a range of organisations in your local area.

You may be able to book a place yourself or you may need a referral from your public health nurse, GP or social worker. Some programmes are free to attend.

How to choose a parenting programme

- Check that it is an accredited (officially recognised) programme given by trained practitioners. Many groups have websites and their accreditation details should be published here.
- Talk to your public health nurse or GP about programmes that are available in your area.
- Contact the person delivering the programme and ask questions about it.
- Ask friends and family about local parenting programmes.

Barnardos has a national database of parenting courses at barnardos.ie. You can search for parenting courses in your local area at barnardos.ie

There are books, DVDs, podcasts and websites that give tips and ideas to make parenting easier. Your local library may have a section on parenting.

Getting help for smoking and alcohol

Keep your home smoke-free and do not smoke around your child as it is bad for their health.

Quitting smoking is one of the best ways to protect your own health and wellbeing. Free help and support that can double your chances of quitting is available from the HSE on quit.ie

For advice on alcohol and your health, see askaboutalcohol.ie

Feeding your child

Eating healthily is about enjoying lots of different healthy foods from the four main food groups, using the children's food pyramid as a guide.

Healthy eating

Healthy eating habits can last a lifetime. Lead by example. If you eat a variety of healthy foods, your child will be more likely to do the same.

Small tummies need small servings. Offer your child three small meals and two to three healthy snacks every day. Children of this age grow and develop fast. All of their food and drink needs to be nourishing.

The children's food pyramid is for children aged 1 to 4. It shows how many daily servings your child should have from each shelf. There are examples of child-size servings on each shelf. Offer your child the number of servings suitable for their age.

Child-sized portions

Use your child's appetite as a guide to help you decide how much food to offer them. Appetite can increase according to your child's growth. Smaller younger children will eat less. Older taller children will eat more. Children who are more physically active will eat more.

Here are some tips on portions:

- Give your child a portion that matches their size. Use the children's food pyramid a guide.
- Do not give your child the same amount of food as you – they are much smaller than you.
- Do not give your child large portions – even if you are giving them healthy food. Large portions can lead to your child becoming overweight.
- Don't put pressure on them to eat all the food on their plate. Allow them to stop when they say "I've had enough".
- Use child-size cutlery, plates and bowls.

20cm	26cm
Child or side plate	Adult's plate
11cm	16cm
Child's bowl	Adult's bowl

Vitamin D – new advice for parents

All children aged 1 to 4 years need a vitamin D supplement during the winter for healthy bones and teeth.

Give 5 micrograms vitamin D only (drops or liquid) every day from Halloween (31st October) to St Patrick's Day (17th March).

Foods and drinks high in fat, sugar and salt

⚠️ **Maximum once a week and in TINY amounts**
These foods can be linked to childhood obesity.

Fats, spreads and oils

Meat, poultry, fish, eggs, beans and nuts

Milk, yogurt and cheese

Vegetables, salad and fruit

Cereals and breads, potatoes, pasta and rice

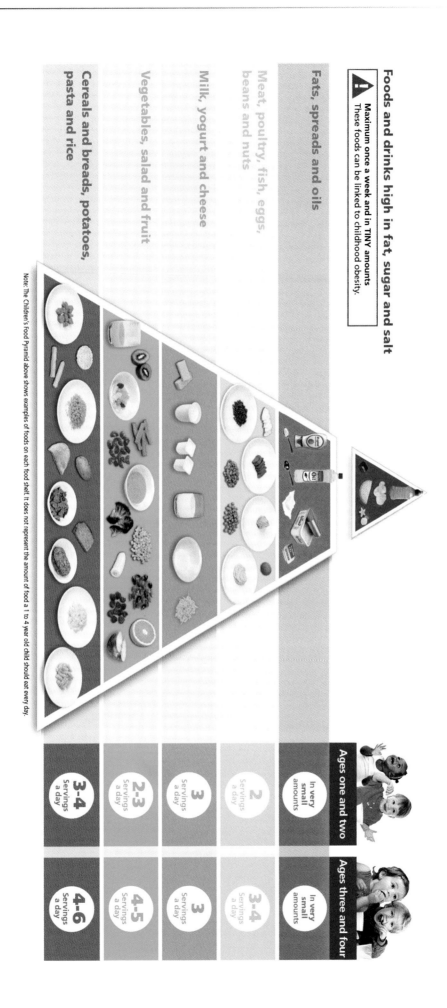

Note: The Children's Food Pyramid above shows examples of foods on each food shelf. It does not represent the amount of food a 1 to 4 year old child should eat every day.

	Ages one and two	Ages three and four
Fats, spreads and oils	In very small amounts	In very small amounts
Meat, poultry, fish, eggs, beans and nuts	2 Servings a day	3-4 Servings a day
Milk, yogurt and cheese	3 Servings a day	3 Servings a day
Vegetables, salad and fruit	2-3 Servings a day	4-5 Servings a day
Cereals and breads, potatoes, pasta and rice	3-4 Servings a day	4-6 Servings a day

17

What is a serving?

Go to www.mychild.ie/nutrition for a full list of suggested servings for each of the main food groups.

Cereals and breads, potatoes, pasta and rice

Age 1 to 2 years: 3 to 4 servings a day
Age 3 to 4 years: 4 to 6 servings a day

Cereals and breads, potatoes, pasta and rice are at the bottom of the children's food pyramid. This is because children need more of these carbohydrate foods for energy and growth.

1 serving is half a cup of pasta

Offer cereals and breads, potatoes, pasta and rice at each meal. This can include pitta bread, wraps, crackers, rice cakes, porridge, flake-type cereals, potatoes, couscous, pasta, plain noodles and rice.

Iron at breakfast time

Offer your child a breakfast cereal with added iron most days of the week. This is especially important for younger children.

Porridge is a healthy breakfast food and children under 5 will benefit from a porridge or cereal with added iron. Check the label and choose cereals and porridge that contain at least 12mg of iron per 100g. Add some fruit rich in vitamin C, which helps your child to absorb iron. For example, chopped berries, kiwi and orange segments.

Limit sugar-coated and-chocolate coated breakfast cereals.

Vegetables, salad and fruit

Age 1 to 2 years: 2 to 3 servings a day
Age 3 to 4 years: 4 to 5 servings a day

Vegetables, salad and fruit provide lots of vitamins, minerals and fibre. These can be fresh or frozen. Tinned fruit in its own juice and vegetables are also nutritious – check the label to make sure there is no added sugar or salt.

1 serving is 3 to 4 cooked carrot sticks

Offer vegetables, salad or fruit at every meal and as snacks. A serving size that fits into half the palm of your hand is about right for your child.

Dried fruits

Dried fruits are not good for teeth as they contain sugar and tend to stick to teeth. These include raisins, apricots, prunes and dates. If giving dried fruits, serve as part of a meal.

Fruit juices

Fruit juices are not recommended. They can damage your child's teeth. All fruit juices are acidic and contain sugar. This includes those with 'no added sugar' written on the label. If you choose to give them, they should be well-diluted and given only with meals.

Offer your child different coloured vegetables, salad and fruit. Try to include green, yellow, orange, red and purple. This will allow them to enjoy the variety of vitamins and minerals. You can add chopped fruit to breakfast cereal.

Milk, yogurt and cheese

Age 1 to 2 years: 3 servings a day
Age 3 to 4 years: 3 servings a day

Milk, yogurt and cheese provide calcium for healthy bones and teeth. Offer these foods three times a day.

Breastfeeding mothers can add cow's milk to their child's cereal or offer cow's milk as a drink. It is important to include yogurt and cheese also to help meet your child's nutritional needs.

1 serving is two adult thumbs of cheese

Follow-on or toddler milks are not necessary. Nutritious foods are better sources of extra nutrients. You can introduce low fat milk after two years of age, if your child is a good eater and has a varied diet. Skimmed milk is not suitable for children under five years.

Soya and other milks

You can give your child soya milk if they are allergic to cow's milk. Soy milk should be unsweetened and fortified with calcium. Almond milk, coconut milk, rice milk and other plant based milks are not suitable for young children.

If your child does not like milk, cheese or yoghurt, try:

- adding grated cheese to pasta or mashed potato
- adding milk to mashed potato
- a cheesy sauce
- homemade pizzas with a wrap or pitta bread and grated cheese
- giving grated cheese as a snack

Breastfeeding support

If you are continuing to breastfeed your child, information and support is available through your local public health nurse or breastfeeding support group such as Cuidiú (cuidiu.ie) or the La Leche League (lalecheleagueireland.com).

The HSE has a free 'Ask the Breastfeeding Expert' service and webchat for breastfeeding questions. See mychild.ie

Meat, fish, eggs, nuts, beans, lentils and tofu

Age 1 to 2 years: 2 servings a day
Age 3 to 4 years: 3 to 4 servings a day

These provide protein and iron for growth and development. Offer twice a day.

Red meats such as beef, lamb and pork contain iron. They should be offered 3 times a week. You should limit processed meat like ham or bacon to once a week and only give small amounts.

1 serving is 30g cooked beef

Oily fish such as mackerel, herring, salmon, trout and sardines have Omega 3 and vitamin D. These are good for brain and eye development. Offer them once a week. This can be cooked or tinned fish. Avoid ones tinned in brine or salt.

An average serving for a child of cooked beef, lamb, pork, chicken, turkey or fish is around 30g. This is about one third the size of an adult's palm of the hand.

> 1 to 3-year-olds who are small for their age may need extra iron. Talk to your public health nurse, GP practice nurse or GP for advice.

> Do not give whole nuts to children under the age of 5 because they may choke. Nuts and seeds should be crushed or ground. Sugar-free and salt-free pure nut butter spreads on bread make a healthy and nutritious lunch. Spread evenly and not too thickly.

Fats, oils and spreads

They should be used sparingly. Always cook with as little fat or oil as possible.

Try to grill, oven-bake, steam, boil or stir-fry. Choose rapeseed, olive, canola, sunflower or corn oils. Limit mayonnaise, coleslaw and salad dressings as they contain oil.

Foods and drinks high in fat, sugar or salt

Limit 'treat' foods. Sweets, chocolate, biscuits, cakes, fizzy drinks and crisps should not be part of your child's daily diet. Having these foods spoils your child's appetite for more nutritious food. They can be linked to childhood obesity.

Sugary foods and drinks can damage your child's teeth. Milk and water are the most tooth-friendly drinks. Do not give your child more than 600ml of milk a day.

Never use foods high in fat, sugar or salt as a reward or to comfort your child. If you decide to give your child these foods, offer them in tiny amounts and only once a week.

Frozen pizza can be high in fat so limit it to a very small slice once a week. Takeaways can be high in fat and salt. They should not be part of your child's diet.

Healthy snack options include fresh fruit, vegetables, plain yogurt, cheese and bread.

A healthy and balanced diet

What to give them

Encourage your child to eat a variety of foods. Their diet will be more balanced when they eat a wide range of different foods.

Encourage them to eat at least five portions of fruit and vegetables daily. Fruit and vegetables contain lots of vitamin A, C and E. See makeastart.ie for healthy eating recipes.

Have a daily routine

Have a regular daily routine. Having regular times for meals and snacks. Avoid grazing throughout the day. This sets up healthy eating habits for life, like starting every day with a healthy breakfast.

Sit down together

Eat with your child as often as possible and praise your child when they eat well.

Screen-free meal times

Try to make meal times relaxed – turn off the television, tablet or phone.

Safety at mealtimes

Never leave your child alone while they are eating in case they choke. Encourage them to sit at the table or to sit still while eating. Children can choke on food if they are walking or running around while they eat.

If you are using a high chair, make sure that your child is securely strapped into it using a five-point harness.

Always remove your child's bib after they have eaten. Bibs can be a strangulation risk.

How to prevent your child from choking on food

Keep foods that your child could choke on out of sight and reach.

Never give your child the following foods as they could choke:

- whole nuts
- marshmallows
- chewing gum
- boiled sweets
- popcorn

Some foods need to be prepared safely (see pages 23 and 117) before you give them to your child.

These include:

- hot dogs and sausages
- raw carrots
- apples and pears
- grapes and similarly shaped fruit and vegetables like cherry tomatoes and soft fruits
- vegetables with leaves
- thick pastes and spreads like peanut butter and chocolate spread

Food choking risks

Always cut food to a size that your child can chew and eat safely.

Offer your child food that matches their age, developmental stage and ability to chew.

If you need to make chewing easier, change the texture of the food – grate, cook, finely chop or mash it.

Remove the parts of food that could choke your child – peel off the skin or remove any strong fibres.

Cut grapes, cherry tomatoes and fruit of a similar shape and soft texture in two lengthways and then into quarters. See page 117 for advice on foods like sausages, hot dogs, carrots, celery, apples, pears, vegetables with leaves, peanut butter and chocolate spread.

How to help your child to be a healthy weight

A healthy and balanced diet

Make sure your child has a healthy balanced diet (see page 16). Eating too much food that is high in sugar, fat and salt is not good for your child's health.

Try not to eat sugary foods yourself and especially not in front of your child.

Enough sleep

Make sure that your child gets enough sleep. Children who don't get enough sleep may be at increased risk of becoming overweight. See tips on helping your child get to sleep on page 30.

Involve them in preparing meals

Involve your children in planning and preparing meals – they are more likely to eat foods they've helped prepare.

Portion size

Keep an eye on portion size. Your child's portions need to be a lot smaller than an adult's portions. See safefood.eu for advice on portion sizes.

Regular mealtimes

Try and have regular mealtimes where you all sit down to eat a healthy balanced meal together. When your child sees you eating lots of different healthy foods, they are more likely to do the same. Make meal times a screen-free zone.

What drinks to give

Offer your child water or milk to drink. You can give your child low fat milk from 2 years old. See page 19. Drinks that are high in sugar such as fizzy drinks are bad for your child's health and their teeth. They can also lead to them becoming overweight. Fruit juices are not recommended. See page 18.

Be active

Encourage your child and your family to be active. Lead by example. Walk with your child rather than use the car or bus if you can. Encourage play time and limit the amount of time your child watches TV and screens.

See makeastart.ie for tips and advice on changing habits and making changes to help your child on the way to a healthier life.

Helping your child stay active

Being active can help your child to have a healthy body, develop self-confidence and improve learning and attention.

Did you know?

Children under five years should have at least three hours of physical activity each day. This can be broken up into little chunks throughout the day. By the time your child reaches five years of age, this should include at least one hour of energetic play. All activity counts – walking, running, dancing, hopping, skipping or cycling.

Ideas for active living:

✔ Create safe places to play.

✔ Play music and learn action songs together.

✔ Dress for the weather and explore the outdoors.

✔ Make time for play with other children.

✔ Whenever possible, get where you're going by walking or cycling.

Staying fit and healthy is important for your child's normal growth and development. It also helps you and your family keep well. Physical exercise and a healthy balanced diet with enough sleep are all part of staying fit and healthy.

A healthy balanced diet and an active life will:

- reduce the risk (see page 23) of your child being overweight or obese
- build strong bones and teeth
- reduce stress and tension by allowing your child to burn off energy
- give them more opportunities to learn and to develop their brain

See page 103 for ideas on toys, fun games and activities that help your child to have an active life.

You can find more advice and information on events in your area on getirelandactive.ie. See makeastart.ie for tips on getting your child physically active.

Children who are overweight or obese

Overweight means that your child weighs more than might be expected for their height. Parents don't always realise when their child is overweight. Your child may not look particularly heavy but might still be overweight.

Obese is a medical term. This describes children who are very overweight and have too much body fat. One in four children in Ireland is overweight or obese.

Risks to health

Being overweight or obese can cause health problems for your child in later life. Children who are overweight or obese tend to grow up to be adults who are overweight or obese.

Short-term risks:

- Poor self-esteem
- Risk of being bullied
- Breathing difficulties
- Problems with bone health

Long-term risks:

- Diabetes
- High blood pressure
- High cholesterol
- Stroke
- Heart disease
- Arthritis
- Mental health problems like depression

What to do if you think your child is overweight or obese

If your child appears to be gaining weight much faster than they should, they may be overweight or obese.

Encourage them to make healthy changes along with the rest of the family (see pages 23 and 24). This will benefit everyone and keep the focus on health rather than on body weight or shape.

Remember your actions may affect your child's future attitudes to food, their body and their self-esteem. What is important is that you support and love your child.

The good food choices you make for your child today will positively affect their health in the future.

Act as a role model by making changes to your own life. For example, by eating healthily, being more active and spending less time watching TV or on your phone.

Get advice from your public health nurse, GP or GP practice nurse about your child's weight. They may refer you to a HSE community dietitian.

Tips for managing foods that are high in sugar, fat and salt

Cut down on foods that are high in sugar, fat and salt such as chocolate, sweets and crisps but don't ban them. In the long run, it's kinder to say no.

It is better if these foods are not part of your weekly shopping. If you have a supply of them at home, keep them out of sight.

Limit the amounts of these foods by:

- getting into the habit of only having them occasionally
- keeping portions small
- offering healthy alternatives

Tell family, friends and everybody who cares for your child that you're making changes to what your family eats.

Alternatives

Say the kitchen is closed when mealtimes are over but allow them to have fruit, chopped vegetables, salad and water.

Don't use food as a reward. Instead praise them and offer non-food treats like a game of football or a trip to the playground.

See makeastart.ie for more advice.

Common questions

Why doesn't my child sit down and eat at mealtimes?

Young children may find it hard to sit down quietly for long periods, especially if mealtimes are long. Be realistic about how long your child can sit quietly. Your child may like some foods more than others. Their favourite food may not be on the menu today, so they lose interest in the meal. Your child's appetite can vary from day to day. We all have days when we are not that hungry.

Children often get extra attention when they do not eat or sit down during mealtime. Your child might realise that their behaviour attracts your attention, so they may repeat it. Instead of coaxing them to eat or getting cross with them, praise their good behaviour. For example, say something like: "You sat through the whole meal tonight. Well done, I like it when you sit nicely with us."

As your child grows and learns good eating habits, they will not act up and behave badly. Continue to praise your child for eating and behaving well at mealtimes.

What can I do about fussy, faddy or picky eating habits?

Fussy, faddy and picky eating is a phase when your child doesn't eat well or refuses to eat certain foods. Children's appetites differ greatly.

Don't be upset if they refuse to eat well on any one day. This is a part of growing up, but it can be very worrying for you as a parent. If this fussy eating continues, ask for advice from your public health nurse, GP, GP practice nurse or pharmacist.

Causes of fussy eating

Your child may be:

- unwell now — or they have been unwell in the recent past
- eating too many snacks between meals
- drinking too much milk or other drinks
- showing their independence

For tips on dealing with your child's behaviour, see page 85.

What foods can I give my child if they are vegetarian?

Make sure that your child gets a healthy balanced diet for their growing body and brain.

Your child needs:

- pulses such as peas, lentils and beans
- milk and milk products, such as yoghurt and cheese

- eggs
- soya foods
- green leafy vegetables, fortified breakfast cereals and vitamin C for iron.

Vegetable sources of iron are not as easily absorbed as animal sources (red meat) but eating a food high in vitamin C with these foods will help your child absorb the iron. Vitamin C foods include oranges, kiwis, peppers and strawberries.

You can get more advice from your HSE community dietitian. Your public health nurse or GP can organise this.

What is a food allergy?

A food allergy is a reaction in your child's immune system to a food they have eaten. Symptoms may appear within minutes (immediate food allergy) or take several hours to appear (delayed food allergy). Food allergies usually happen very early in life.

The symptoms of immediate food allergy usually appear the first time your child eats the food. The most common immediate food allergies are to nuts, eggs and milk. The most common delayed food allergy is cow's milk allergy which begins when a child is a baby. Toddlers do not develop milk allergy for the first time. Similarly children aged 2 to 5 years do not develop wheat allergy.

Diagnosing a food allergy

If you think your child may have a food allergy, talk to your GP or your public health nurse. Don't eliminate foods from your child's diet without getting expert advice. If your child is already eating milk, wheat, eggs and nuts then they do not need allergy tests to these foods. The only tests that will accurately diagnose a food allergy are the ones done by your GP or in hospital.

Mythbusters

Drinking milk and eating dairy products does not lead to mucus in the nose, throat and lungs. Lactose intolerance is not a food allergy. It is a problem related to difficulty breaking down sugar in the milk. Coeliac disease is not a food allergy. The symptoms can start between the ages of 2 and 5 years.

Symptoms

Symptoms of immediate food allergy
- Hives (nettle sting type rash).
- Swelling around face and eyes.
- Sudden sneezing and nasal blockage.
- Itchy, red or watery eyes.
- Tummy pains or vomiting (with some of the other symptoms).
- More severe symptoms like breathing difficulties or collapse can develop (anaphylaxis) in rare situations. Call 999 or 112 if you think this is happening.

Symptoms of delayed food allergy
Any combination of:

- vomiting
- diarrhoea
- blood in the poo
- reflux
- tummy getting bloated

Most food allergies that cause diarrhoea happen in children younger than 2.

Sleeping

Children need a good night's sleep so they can have plenty of energy for the next day. It is also good for their health and reduces their risk of obesity. Parents need some adult time and enough sleep themselves.

Every child has a different sleep pattern. You can help your child's development by making sure they are well-rested.

Age	How much sleep your child needs
From about 2 to 3 years old	Your child needs around 11 to 12 hours of sleep a night and one nap of about 30 minutes.
	The length of the nap depends on your child and their activity that day. Try not to let your child nap beyond mid-afternoon. This will help them to be tired and ready for sleep again by night time.
From about 3 to 5 years old	Your child needs around 11 to 12 hours of sleep a night.
	At age three, your child may need one nap during the daytime of about 30 minutes. Not all children need this nap. Some quiet time reading and playing may be enough.
	When your child comes home from preschool or their childminder, they may be very tired because of the routine and activity there. This is especially true when they start attending.

Developing a positive bedtime routine

Their bedroom

Make your child's bedroom a nice and comfortable room that they enjoy spending time in.

Have consistent limits

As a parent you need to set clear limits and boundaries at bedtime. For example, if you say two stories, then stick to this!

Remember that it is natural for children to test boundaries. Many children do this at bedtime. Some resist going to bed while others go to bed but get up repeatedly. Children are most likely to test limits between three to six years.

Bedtime

Make sure that your child has had supper, a small drink and has been to the toilet to avoid requests for this after you have settled them. A bedtime routine including supper should take between 30 to 45 minutes. See page 31 for tips.

Don't put your child to bed too early. A child should fall asleep within 30 minutes of going to bed. You may need to make bedtime later for a while until they can do this. Then gradually bring bedtime back by 15 minutes a night to the bedtime you want. You will need to have the same morning wake-up time for this to work. Anytime between 7pm and 8pm is a good guide to settle your child down for the night.

Have a consistent bedtime routine where there is a regular bedtime. Follow this routine in the same way each night. Your child will then know what to expect.

If they get up

If your child gets up during the night, try to settle them back in their own bed.

Reward them

Reward your child for staying in their own bed. Use a reward chart and have a 'bigger' reward if they get three stickers on their chart. The 'bigger' reward could be an activity like a trip to the library to choose a book.

Be consistent

The key to success is consistency. Keep going even if you meet resistance initially. It will get better.

Quiet time before bedtime

It is important to have a wind-down period for your child before they go to bed. This routine should last 30 to 45 minutes. Here are some tips to help:

✔ Avoid television and screens in the hour before bed.

✔ Give them a supper.

✔ Help them get into pyjamas.

✔ Do some quiet activities such as jigsaws or colouring.

✔ Brush teeth, go to the toilet and get washed.

✔ Do story-time and say goodnight.

✔ Tuck them into bed and turn off the lights.

✔ If your child is afraid of the dark, plug in a dim night light to help them settle.

If you follow a consistent bedtime schedule in the same way at about the same time each night, it will help your child feel secure and loved. It can help to give them a restful night.

Where your child should sleep

Between the ages of 3 and 5, your child will be ready to move into a low bed. Sometimes you may need to make this change sooner. For example, if your child:

- is climbing out of the cot
- grows too big for their cot

You need to childproof your child's bedroom. You will need to do this regularly as they grow. It is especially important to make sure the room is childproof when they move into their own bed as they will then be able to get up and move freely around their room when they wake up. See page 111.

Children should be at least six years old before they are allowed to sleep on the top bunk of a bunk bed.

Naps

Each child has a different need for sleep and a different pattern of napping. For some children, quiet time reading a book or playing quietly is all that they need. For others, a nap is still important to stop them becoming cross and cranky.

- Set up a daily routine so your child knows when the nap is due each day.
- Keep your child's bed for sleeping only, not for playing or relaxing.
- Close the curtains so the room is darkened.
- Remove your child's shoes and outer clothes, such as a heavy jumper, so they do not become too warm when they sleep.
- Give them their special blanket or soft toy as a comforter in bed. Don't put anything into your child's cot or bed that they could choke on or could suffocate or strangle them.
- Speak in a calm tone of voice if you are reading a short story to them.
- When the nap is over, try to let your child wake up on their own. If they wake themselves, they will be in a better mood and ready to get active again.
- Avoid naps after 3.30pm as this may lead to resistance going to bed later.

Managing sleep problems

Sleep problems are common in preschool children. Night time fears, nightmares, sleepwalking and sleep terrors often first appear in this age group.

Nightmares

Nightmares are dreams that upset or frighten your child. Some children have nightmares now and again. The nightmares may be linked to something that happened during the day or a worry or fear your child has. Worries and fears can include starting preschool, a death in the family or a fear of monsters.

Nightmares generally happen during the last few hours of sleep. When they wake, your child will usually tell you about the dream. They may even think that the dream was real.

As your child gains confidence in dealing with problems, they tend to have fewer nightmares.

How to help your child after a nightmare

Hold and comfort your child when they wake from a nightmare. If your child is too upset to be left alone, sit beside them and reassure them you will be nearby if they need you.

Try to avoid getting into bed beside them. This could become a sleep association they rely on to fall back to sleep each time they wake.

Leave their bedroom door and yours open so they know you are near.

Try to eliminate any daytime worries your child has. For example, encourage your child to talk to you and carefully choose the TV programmes that they watch.

Ask your GP or public health nurse for advice if:

- the nightmare is very disturbing
- it keeps happening for a month or so

Avoid giving your child drinks that contain caffeine like tea, coffee, cola and energy drinks as they can cause disrupted sleep. Energy drinks often have high levels of caffeine and sugar. They are not a suitable drink for your child.

Sleep terrors

Sleep or night terrors occur in the deepest part of sleep and usually within one to two hours of going to bed. Because they occur in sleep, your child will have no memory of them. They are distressing for parents.

Sleep terrors are more likely to occur if your child is not getting enough sleep. A change in routine, like giving up the daytime nap or starting preschool, may trigger a sleep terror.

What to do

The important thing to remember is not to wake them, as this may lead to more agitation.

In most cases sleep terrors do not need treatment and will run their course. The most important thing is to keep your child safe and avoid injury.

Sleep terrors can last from five minutes to 30 minutes and have no effect on your child. They will not remember it the next day. For this reason, it is better not to discuss it with your child as this may cause them to worry. But it may still help to have a general chat with your child to make sure there is nothing worrying them.

When to get help

Most children will grow out of night terrors. Talk to your GP if they are happening several times a night or most nights.

Not sleeping through the night

Settling your child to a sleep pattern takes time. You need to follow the same routine at roughly the same time each night.

Your child's sleep can be disturbed by changes. For example, dropping a nap, starting pre-school or moving from a cot to a bed.

Try not to reward them if they wake at night. Avoid stimulating activities like letting them watch TV.

If possible, settle them back to sleep in their own bed.

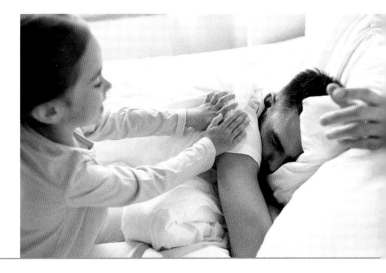

Waking very early in the morning

Many young children wake up early. They usually wake in good spirits and may start chatting or singing.

The problem is that they may move from their bed to greet you or other family members who are sound asleep.

Here are some tips that may help you to manage this.

- Make sure your child is not hungry. It is a good idea to give your child supper before they go to bed.
- Review your child's nap times. If they nap too early, this may lead to tiredness early in the evening.
- Avoid putting your child to bed too early. For example, if your child is asleep by 7pm they may wake at around 5.30am.
- Make sure their sleep schedule is consistent, otherwise it can disrupt their sleep pattern.
- Try to avoid morning light, noise and activity. Morning television can also cause children to get out of bed.

If your child does wake up early and is in good form, then you can adjust the bedtime for a later wakening. For example, if your child goes to bed at 7pm and wakes up at 5am in good form, then they have had 10 hours sleep. You can gradually make bedtime 15 minutes later (7pm, then 7.15pm, then 7.30pm, then 7.45pm and then 8pm).

This takes a few days to work so be consistent and don't give up. This may mean they wake later in the morning. The aim is to have your child asleep from 8pm to 6am, which is more reasonable than 5am.

Bed-wetting
See page 42.

Did you know?

Children who don't get enough sleep may be at increased risk of becoming overweight.

Bedtime tips
- ✔ Encourage children to be active in the evenings to tire them out but have wind down time in the hour before bed.
- ✔ Have a light supper of cereal (low in salt and sugar) or toast and milk.
- ✔ Create a sleep-friendly environment that is dark, quiet, comfortable and cool.
- ✔ Keep your child's bedroom a screen-free zone.

Contact your public health nurse or GP if you are concerned that:

- your child is not sleeping
- their sleep pattern is disturbed

Caring for your child

As your child grows, they can play more of a role in everyday tasks like brushing their teeth and putting on their clothes. They'll need your support and praise to help them grow more independent.

Your child's teeth

Tooth decay is also called dental decay or dental caries. This is the destruction of the hard surfaces of the teeth.

Tooth decay takes place when sugary foods and drinks are broken down by bacteria in the mouth to form acids which destroy the tooth surface. It is the most common ongoing childhood disease. It can be difficult to treat in young children.

Preventing tooth decay

Teeth are at risk of decay as soon as they appear in the mouth. Any foods and drinks that contain sugar can cause decay. Controlling how often your child has sugary foods and drinks is very important to prevent decay.

Delay the introduction of sugary foods and drinks for as long as possible.

How to keep your child's teeth healthy

Encourage your child to eat a balanced diet (see page 16) with plenty of fruit, vegetables and fibre.

Foods and drinks that contain sugar can lead to tooth decay. Keep foods and drinks that contain sugar to mealtimes only. Do not give sugary foods as snacks between meals.

Give milk and water

Milk and water are the most tooth-friendly drinks. They are good drinks to give your child with or between meals. If you choose to offer fruit juice or squash, keep it to meal times only and dilute well.

Avoid fizzy drinks

They contain a lot of sugar and acid. If your child does have a fizzy drink, use a straw. It helps keep the fluid away from their teeth.

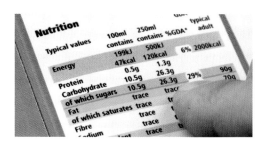

Read food labels carefully

Sugar may also be called sucrose, fructose, glucose or maltose on labels. 'Low sugar' or 'no added sugar' on the label does not mean that the food or drink is sugar-free.

Foods that include sugar substitutes are available but these should be eaten in moderation.

Sugar-free medicines should be used when available.

Bring them to the dentist

Visit your dentist with your child at least once a year.

How to clean your child's teeth

Always help your child with tooth brushing. Brush twice a day, especially at bed-time. Use a soft toothbrush with a small head. It takes about two minutes for your child to brush their teeth properly. Try to make brushing fun.

Toothpaste

Use a small pea-sized amount of fluoride toothpaste. Use regular family toothpaste containing fluoride from age two years. Fluoride gives added protection to teeth.

Children's toothpaste with low fluoride (for example 500 ppm) does not provide as much protection as regular fluoride toothpaste.

Your child should spit out any remaining toothpaste after brushing but should not rinse their mouth out afterwards. If they rinse, the fluoride won't work as well.

Toothbrush

Change your child's toothbrush about every three months or when the bristles get ragged.

> Look out for the first permanent molar teeth coming up at the back of your child's mouth from the age of five. Make sure they include these teeth when they are brushing.

Injuries to teeth

Falls, bangs and bumps are part of the daily life of young children and injuries to teeth can easily happen.

Up to age five, many children will still have all their baby teeth. An injury to the mouth can loosen, break, knock out or push a baby tooth up into the gum. This can damage the developing permanent tooth.

What to do

Take your child to the dentist if they injure a baby tooth or a permanent tooth in a fall or accident.

If your child knocks out a baby tooth, do not try to put the tooth back in place.

Children in this age group are less likely to have a permanent (adult) tooth. If they do knock one out, place the tooth back in its socket and go to the dentist immediately. If you can't put it back in the socket, place it in milk and bring it and your child to the dentist immediately.

See page 65 for more information on caring for your child's teeth.

Washing your child

Bath time

Bath time gives your child a chance to have fun with floating toys, plastic cups, bubbles and warm water.

- Stay close to your child and never leave them alone in the bath.
- Run cold water first, then add the warm water. If your bath has a single tap with a hot and cold feed, make sure you run the cold water again to cool the taps so they won't burn your child.
- Test the bath water temperature with your elbow or bath thermometer before putting your child into the bath. The correct temperature is 37°C to 38°C.
- Make sure your child doesn't turn on the hot tap and scald themselves or slip and fall in the bath or shower.
- Always empty the bath as soon as you remove your child.

Everyday washing

Teach your child to wash their hands:

- before mealtimes
- before and after baking or preparing food with you
- after they use the potty or toilet
- after contact with animals

This will protect your child from infections.

Get a small box or step for them to stand on at the hand basin. The step will also help your child reach other things like their own toothbrush.

> Don't leave dangerous items, such as medication or a razor, where your child can reach them.

Dressing your child

Most active toddlers are well able to take off their clothes, shoes and socks. Encourage your child to do as much as they can for themselves. They will be more likely to let you do the difficult bits such as pulling the jumper over their head.

Teach them to dress themselves

Describe in simple language what you are going to do as you help your child dress. Then repeat the action with them. For example, place your hands over your child's hands as they put on their own vest. Comment on what you are doing. Your child gains confidence as they learn new skills from you.

Teach them to tie their shoelaces or to use Velcro, buckle or elastic-sided shoes.

Let them help choose clothes

Let your child help to decide what clothes they wear. Give your child a choice of two or three sets of clothes that are practical. Let them make the final decision. Praise them for their sense of style.

Allow your child to dress themselves as much as they can as this is an important life skill. It will take time but your child will get quicker as they practice. Praise them for each step as they learn to put on socks, shoes, t-shirts and so on.

What clothes to choose for your child

When your child is a toddler, choose clothes and shoes with Velcro fastenings, elastic or snap fasteners. Buy shoes with laces or buttons when your child is older and can manage laces or buttons themselves.

It is important that your child's shoes or sandals fit correctly. Get your child's feet measured regularly by a trained assistant in a shoe shop.

Be careful with clothes that use a string or cord to tie the hood or waist. They could cause injury if they become caught up in something while your child is playing.

Never place these items on your child:

- hair bands
- jewellery (including amber teething jewellery)
- strings
- cords
- belts
- ribbons
- clips
- ties
- clothes and hats with strings or cords attached

Toilet training your child

Toilet training is also known as potty training. It means teaching your child to go to the toilet by themselves when they are ready to do so.

When you begin toilet training your child, decide at the beginning on the words you are going to use such as 'wee' for passing urine and 'poo' for a bowel motion. Talk about these in a positive way.

How to know when your child is ready

Ask yourself these questions to see if your child is ready to toilet train.

- Can they follow simple directions?
- Is their nappy dry for at least 2 hours at a time during the day?
- Is their nappy dry after a daytime nap?
- Are their bowel movements regular and predictable?
- Can they pull their pants up and down by themselves?
- Do they seem uncomfortable in wet or dirty nappies?
- Do they know the difference between wet and dry?
- Can they tell you that a wee or poo is coming?

If you answer yes to most of these questions, your child is ready to be toilet trained. Children are usually ready for toilet training between two and three years old. But each child starts in their own time.

Start with a potty

You can begin training your child on a small training potty rather than the full-sized toilet. Small children may be afraid of falling into the toilet, especially when the toilet is being flushed.

As your child becomes more comfortable with using the potty, introduce them to a small training seat that clips over the seat of a full-sized toilet.

Your child can use a small step to get up and sit on the training seat.

It is better to train boys in a sitting position first. He may want to poo as well as wee. When he is confident sitting on the potty, you can encourage him to wee standing up.

A training seat and small step

How to toilet train your child

Let your child set the pace for training. Train them when it feels right for them.

Plan to set aside three to four days to begin the toilet training. After that, maintain the same routine in the weeks that follow. For example, start a routine of sitting your child on the potty first thing after meals and naps and before bedtime.

Getting ready

Tell your child that when they are a big girl or boy they will be able to go to the toilet to do their wee and poo. This gives them the opportunity to share the decision about their toilet training.

Start to change your child's nappy in the bathroom all the time as this will help them associate nappy changing with toileting. You can also encourage your child to wash their hands after the nappy change.

Take your child with you when you or your other children go to the toilet. It prepares your child by letting them see what they should do when it is their turn.

Leave the potty nearby. For example, have one upstairs and one downstairs if your home is on two levels.

Plan ahead. If you are going out, bring a few sets of spare pants, soft toilet tissue and baby wipes. If your child is in a crèche, discuss their training needs with the staff.

Put your child in easy-to-care-for clothes that they can pull up and down easily.

Using the potty

Watch your child for signals that they know their wee or poo is coming, such as hopping up and down, holding their pants or hiding. Get them to the potty quickly.

While they are on the potty, let your child look at a book about toilet training or listen to music to help them relax.

Praise your child for every little step. Help your child to manage for themselves on the potty or the toilet, but don't leave them to manage alone. Go with your child when they ask you to.

After they have finished

After they have finished, tell them you are going to wipe their bottom. Remember to wipe girls from front to back to prevent infection.

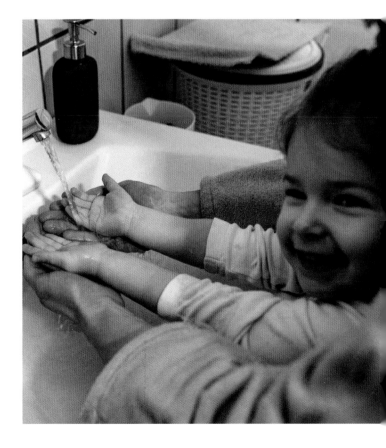

Teach your child to always wash their hands with soap and water after they use the toilet or potty.

Empty the contents of the potty down the toilet. Wash the potty out with warm soapy water and a disinfectant.

Your child may prefer to flush the toilet themselves. Let them. Doing things for themselves helps your child's sense of independence and self-confidence.

Nappies and trainer pants ('pull-ups')

When your child is mostly dry at home, leave off the nappy or trainer pants ('pull-up') during the day and only use them at night.

Although you may still have a number of puddles, giving up nappies or trainer pants encourages your child to use the potty.

Other tips

- Wait until they are old enough to understand your instructions. Every child is different and it's important to go at your child's pace.
- Be patient. Don't force your child to train if they are unhappy or do not want to train. Stop and try again in two to three weeks. Your child will set their own pace.
- Don't force your child to stay on the potty until they wee or poo. If they say they can't, calmly help them off and try later.
- Don't get your child to hold on to a bowel motion. They may not be able to and it is uncomfortable to do so.
- Encourage the behaviour you want by giving your child lots of praise. Try not to get annoyed when they have an accident as this can put them off trying again.
- It is not a good idea to start toilet training if you are about to move home or have a new baby. These big events could upset your child and affect their routine. Wait a few months before you start toilet training.

Using a reward chart

Reward charts are a good way to motivate your child to do something. For example, to reward your child for using the potty, you can stick a star on a big poster of a toilet that you both coloured.

> Make sure to continue to praise your child even if you are using reward charts. There is nothing more important to your child than your love and cuddles.

Don't remove a star from the chart if your child is naughty or has an accident. They earned the reward. Taking it away can discourage them.

Night-time toilet training

Generally night-time control comes months after daytime control. Your child should regularly wake up dry in the morning before you leave off nappies at night. It could take three to four weeks of dry nappies in the morning before you consider leaving a nappy off at night.

Mattress protector

Put a mattress protection cover over the mattress. Let your child know that it doesn't matter if they wet the bed.

Make getting to the toilet easy

Make sure the toilet is easy to reach at night – you may need a night light to help them find the toilet if they wake at night to go.

Food and drink

Encourage them to drink plenty of water or milk only. Avoid fizzy drinks, tea and coffee as they stimulate their bladder and increase the need to wee. They should drink water and no more than 600ml of milk throughout the day and up until bedtime.

There is no benefit to stopping drinks after 6pm. Stopping drinks does not encourage a healthy bladder and it can dehydrate your child.

Make sure they eat plenty of fruit, vegetables, salad and wholegrain breakfast cereals, bread, pasta and rice to prevent constipation.

Before they go to bed

A regular bedtime routine and avoiding screens before bedtime will help encourage a healthy pattern of sleep and help your child to become dry at night.

Make sure your child goes to the toilet before they go to sleep.

After bed-wetting

If the bed is wet, involve your child in changing the bed and night clothes. Encourage them to shower or bathe in the morning to avoid having wee on their body.

Many young children stay dry all night with no problems and few accidents. But most children are not reliably dry before their fifth birthday and 15% of 5-year-olds regularly wet the bed.

Even after the age of five, occasional bed-wetting is common. Lifting a child to go for a wee late at night is not a great idea. Your child is very sleepy and lifting them doesn't help them take charge when they feel like going to the toilet themselves.

Remember that toilet training takes time. It is very important for you to be as patient and encouraging as possible. Praise their effort and not the result!

Contact your public health nurse if you need advice.

If your child was dry at night but now wets the bed again

If your child has been dry for over six months and they start bedwetting again, they may be reacting to stress in their daily life.

Reasons for this may include:

- A new baby in the family.
- A separation from you or another main carer.
- Starting a new school.
- Bullying.
- The death of someone close, such as a grandparent.
- Any other major upheaval in their routine can shake your child's confidence.

They may stop their more grown-up behaviour for a while and may have trouble sleeping. They might ask for a soother, breastfeed or bottle.

What to do

Reassure your child to help them cope with change. You can get advice from your public health nurse or GP. They may refer your child to a specialist if more help is needed.

When an older child wets the bed

Night-time bedwetting in a child who is five years and older is also called enuresis. Night-time bedwetting is very common until your child is around five years old and it is not unusual up to the age of seven, especially in boys.

Don't be in a hurry to decide that your child has a problem. Many young children simply grow out of night-time bedwetting. But waiting for an improvement can be a stressful time for you and your family.

Many parents find it difficult not to worry about wet beds when their child is four, five or six. It's best to keep calm and support your child.

Did you know?

Bedwetting in older children is more common than you think. One in seven children aged five years and one in 20 children aged 10 years wet the bed at night. You are not alone in dealing with bedwetting.

Why your older child still wets the bed at night

There are a number of reasons why your older child may still wet the bed.

- Bedwetting can run in families.
- Sometimes your child sleeps through the signal of a full bladder.
- Some children produce large amounts of wee during the night.
- Your child's bladder could be small and less able to hold a lot of wee.

Other times to see your GP

If your child has:

- signs of a urinary tract infection, such as pain when weeing or a temperature of 38°C or higher
- signs of constipation, such as pains in their tummy, pooing less frequently than usual or passing small amounts of hard poo
- been wetting themselves during the day
- been dry at night for a while and suddenly starts wetting the bed again

Don't expect a miracle cure for wet beds. Becoming dry at night will come gradually.

If it doesn't, contact:

- your public health nurse
- your GP
- your GP practice nurse

Head lice and nits

Head lice and nits are very common in children. They can happen to anyone and have nothing to do with how clean their hair is.

Head lice are tiny insects that lay eggs. Eggs hatch after seven to 10 days. Nits are the yellow, brown or white empty shells left behind after the egg hatches. They are tiny and look a bit like dandruff. Unlike dandruff, they do not brush out easily.

How children and adults catch head lice

You can catch head lice by holding your head against someone who has head lice. Head lice don't jump or fly, they walk from one head to another. They can occasionally be passed by sharing brushes, combs and hats. Lice don't live for long in clothes or bedding.

Signs your child has head lice

If your child has head lice you may notice them scratching their head. Most children won't have an itch. The only way to be sure they have lice is by finding live lice or eggs.

How to check your child's hair

'Wet comb' your child's hair with a special fine-toothed detection comb that you can get from your pharmacy or online. Wet comb simply means combing through your child's wet hair.

How to 'wet comb' your child's hair

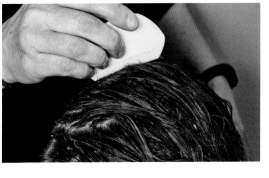

1. Wash your child's hair with ordinary shampoo.
2. Dry it with a towel, the hair should be damp, not dripping wet.
3. If your child's hair is tangled, use a little conditioner.
4. Comb through your child's hair with an ordinary comb.
5. Using the detection comb, slot the teeth of the comb into the hair at the roots and pull the comb down to the ends.
6. Check the comb for lice every time you do this. Make sure there is good light. Daylight is the best and a magnifying glass may help.
7. Repeat this several times. Each time, go from the top of the head to the edge of the hair. Go in all directions, working round the head.
8. After the whole head has been combed, rinse off any conditioner you applied.

It takes 10 to 15 minutes to comb through your child's head properly. It's a good idea to get into a routine of doing this about once a week.

What to do if you find lice in your child's hair

1. Check everyone else who lives in the home (including parents).
2. Treat your child and anyone else with lice on the same day.
3. Talk to anyone who has been in close contact with your child so they can check themselves and their children.
4. There is no need to keep your child home from school.

Anyone with moving and living lice in their hair needs to be treated.

How to treat lice

You can treat lice yourself at home. You don't need to bring your child to the GP.

The best way to treat head lice is with a special medicated lotion. You can buy this over the counter at your pharmacy. Get advice and follow the instructions carefully.

If you or your child still has lice after treatment

This could be due to:

- re-infection
- the treatment not working or not being carried out correctly

Check the whole family again, and treat everyone who has lice again.

If you still find lice after this, talk to your GP or pharmacist.

Preventing head lice

There is nothing you can do to prevent lice. If your child has long hair, tying it back may help.

Don't use the lotion "just in case". Only use the treatment if you find living, moving lice. The treatments are safe but they shouldn't be over-used. They can sometimes irritate the scalp.

Things you shouldn't use to treat lice:

- ✗ Tea tree oil and other plant-based oils (eucalyptus or lavender)
- ✗ Electric combs
- ✗ Head lice 'repellents'
- ✗ Permethrin-containing products

These products are not recommended because they won't work.

Vaccines (immunisation)

When your child is in junior infants they should have the following vaccinations:

- 4-in-1 to protect against diphtheria, whooping cough (pertussis), tetanus and polio
- a second dose of MMR to protect against measles, mumps and rubella (German measles)

These vaccines are provided free-of-charge by the HSE.

Your child will receive an information pack about the vaccine from their school offering 4-in-1 and MMR vaccines. In Sligo, Leitrim and Donegal, the 4-in-1 and MMR vaccines are given by your GP.

From time to time, the HSE may introduce new vaccines, booster vaccination campaigns and catch-up programmes. You will be notified by the HSE (usually by letter) if your child needs further vaccines at any stage.

If your child misses their vaccination appointment, contact the HSE school team. They will usually arrange for your child to attend a 'catch-up clinic'.

See immunisation.ie for more information.

When your child is sick

Most children get ill at some stage. Usually you can care for them at home, as most illnesses pass quickly. Contact your GP if you are unsure what to do or worried about your child.

When to get urgent medical help

When to call an ambulance

You should always call 112 or 999 if your child is seriously ill or injured, or their life is at risk.

Examples of medical emergencies include (but are not limited to):

- difficulty breathing
- unconsciousness
- severe loss of blood
- severe burns or scalds
- choking
- having a fit or convulsion that lasts for more than five minutes
- severe head injury
- drowning
- severe allergic reactions

Directions and Eircode

It is a good idea to make a list of easy-to-follow directions to your home and put them in a visible place.

Eircodes may help the ambulance service to find you faster. Make a note of your home's Eircode and put it somewhere obvious in case you need to give it out in emergency. See eircode.ie if you need to check your Eircode.

When to contact your GP or hospital emergency department

Always contact your GP or hospital emergency department if your child:

- has a purple or red rash that looks unusual
- has a raised or sunken soft spot (fontanelle) on the front top of their head
- has a fever of 39°C or higher
- appears much paler and sleepier then usual and is hard to wake up
- has an unusual, non-stop, high pitched cry or scream

- has had a fit (convulsion)
- has difficulty breathing
- goes blue around the lips or face
- is not drinking fluids
- is not weeing as much as usual or their wee is a dark colour
- has diarrhoea for more than 24 hours
- has bloody diarrhoea
- has a bad fall or a bump on the head
- gets an electric shock
- is burned or scalded
- is bitten by an animal

Poison

If you think that your child has taken poison, stay calm but act quickly.

Contact the Poisons Information Helpline by ringing 01 809 2166 (save this number to your phone). Your call will be answered by a specialist who will tell you if your child needs medical attention.

The helpline is open from 8am to 10pm every day. Outside of these hours, contact your GP or hospital. In an emergency call 112 or 999. See poisons.ie for more information.

Common childhood illnesses

Most children get ill at some stage. Usually, you can care for them at home, as these illnesses pass quickly.

Over the next few pages, we list some common childhood illnesses and advise on what you should do. If you are unsure, contact your GP.

Fever

A fever is a high temperature of 38°C or higher. Most of the time, viral infections like colds and flus cause high temperatures. However, sometimes a high temperature can be a sign that your child has a more serious infection, like meningitis (see page 57).

What to do

To help reduce your child's temperature, encourage them to drink lots of fluids such as water or milk. You may also need to give your child extra drinks to prevent dehydration. Remove their outer clothes to allow extra heat to escape from their body.

You can give medications such as liquid paracetamol or ibuprofen to lower your child's temperature. But if they are comfortable and appear well, they may not need medicine. If you do give your child paracetamol or ibuprofen, always read the instructions. Keep all medicines out of sight and reach of children.

Always get advice from your GP if your child:

- has a temperature of 39°C or higher
- is showing other signs of being unwell such as drowsiness, refusing to eat or drink or persistent vomiting

Febrile convulsion

A febrile convulsion or seizure is sometimes called a fit. It can happen if your child has a high temperature. The febrile convulsion may last for several minutes. Afterwards your child may be sleepy and limp.

During a febrile convulsion, your child may:

- become stiff and their arms and legs may begin to jerk
- lose consciousness
- wet or soil themselves
- foam at the mouth or vomit
- turn blue
- roll back their eyes

What to do

To help your child:

1. Note the time that the convulsion started.
2. Lie your child on one side with their head tilted back slightly. This makes sure that their airway stays clear and that your child will not swallow any vomit.
3. Do not put anything in your child's mouth.
4. Do not try to restrain them or shake them.
5. When the seizure stops, try to lower your child's temperature (see page 48). Make sure the room is warm but remove outer layers of clothing. This will help your child feel more comfortable.

Call an ambulance by ringing 999 or 112 if:

- a seizure lasts for more than five minutes
- another seizure begins soon after the first one ends

Seeing your child have a febrile convulsion can be very frightening. But they are usually harmless and most children make a full recovery.

Although there is unlikely to be anything seriously wrong with your child, it is still important to bring them to a hospital emergency department that treats children.

Croup

Croup is common in young children up to the age of three. It is caused by a virus. Your child may have a barking cough, be hoarse or make a harsh sound when breathing.

What to do

Croup usually gets better on its own after 48 hours. It can be very stressful for parents. Try to stay calm in front of your child. Your child may panic and find it harder to breathe if they sense that you are stressed.

- Reassure them and comfort them.
- Keep them upright and don't let them lie down.
- Give them fluids to drink such as water.
- Don't give them any cough medicine, any herbal remedies or any medications that haven't been prescribed.
- Don't put your child in a steamy room or get them to inhale steam.

When to get medical help

The symptoms of croup are often mild, but they can become severe and things can change quickly. Sometimes children need to be admitted to hospital for treatment of their croup. For this reason you should always bring your child to the GP if you think they have croup.

If their symptoms are severe or if they are finding it hard to breathe, bring them to your nearest hospital emergency department that treats children.

Coughs and colds

To help stop coughs and colds from spreading:

- wash your hands often
- use tissues to trap germs when your child coughs or sneezes and bin them straight away
- teach your child to cough into the crook of their arm

Most coughs are caused by viruses like colds and flus. There is no quick way of getting rid of a cough, which can often last for up to 21 days.

What to do

Once your child is drinking fluids and is in fairly good form they can usually be cared for at home. Give them plenty of fluids to drink and offer food as usual.

If your child's nose is blocked you can wipe it gently. Saline drops can also help. Talk to your pharmacist before using them.

If your child has a fever or if they are uncomfortable, children's paracetamol or ibuprofen can help to settle them. Always check the instructions on the packet before you give medicine to a child.

A warm and moist atmosphere can also help. Try taking your child into the bathroom where you have run a hot bath or shower. Make sure to keep your child away from the hot water so they are not at risk of being scalded. You could also use a humidifier to moisten the air. Position this in a safe place where children cannot reach it.

Contact your GP if your child:

- has symptoms which last for more than three weeks
- is getting worse rather than better
- is rubbing or pulling at their ears and seems irritable
- seems wheezy (making noise when they are breathing)
- is refusing to drink fluids
- shows any other worrying symptoms

> If your child is finding it hard to breathe, then get medical help urgently from your GP or nearest hospital emergency department that treats children.

Ear infection

An ear infection is usually caused by a virus. Most ear infections will clear up on their own after three to four days.

Signs that your child has an ear infection may include:

- a temperature
- irritability and restlessness
- touching or pulling at the ear
- complaining of earache and reduced hearing (older children)
- having no interest in eating or drinking

What to do

To help your child:

- Do not use a cotton bud or anything else to poke inside their ear, as it may cause damage and pain.
- Give children's paracetamol or ibuprofen to reduce the pain (always read the instructions).

Take your child to the GP if:

- you are worried
- there is a discharge from the ear
- they seem very unwell, drowsy, or
- they are not taking fluids

Antibiotics do not work against viral infections. They will not reduce the pain of an ear infection. Your GP will only prescribe an antibiotic if they feel your child's ear infection has been caused by bacteria.

Tummy upsets (gastroenteritis)

If your child has a tummy upset with vomiting, diarrhoea or both, then they can get dehydrated (dried out). Make sure you give them enough to drink.

What to do

Fluids

Give them enough to drink in small sips. Small sips of clear fluid work best.

If your child is beginning to show mild signs of dehydration, ask your GP or pharmacist if you should be giving them oral rehydration solution. This is a special powder that you make into a drink. It contains sugar and salts to help replace the water and salts lost through vomiting and diarrhoea.

Food

Don't worry too much about food. Fluids are the most important thing while your child is ill. If your child hasn't lost their appetite, it's fine for them to eat solid foods as normal.

Liquid paracetamol

If they are uncomfortable and have a high temperature or tummy pains, you can give your child liquid paracetamol. Always read the liquid paracetamol label to make sure you give the correct dose to your child. Keep all medicines out of your child's sight and reach.

Signs of dehydration

Look out for signs of dehydration — such as not wetting many nappies, having a dry mouth, being drowsy or having no tears.

Contact your GP if your child:

- is not drinking fluids or has any signs of dehydration
- has blood in their poo
- has had six or more episodes of diarrhoea in the past 24 hours, or three or more episodes of vomiting

The 48 hour rule

Children with vomiting should not attend a crèche, childminder or school until at least 48 hours after their last vomit.

Children with diarrhoea should not attend a crèche, childminder or school until 48 hours after their poo gets back to normal.

Wash your hands regularly to avoid spreading any illness.

VTEC

VTEC (Verotoxigenic E. coli) is a serious type of gastroenteritis that can cause complications such as kidney failure.

A child infected with VTEC may have:

- diarrhoea (this could be bloody)
- stomach pains
- high temperature

About one in 10 children with VTEC can develop serious complications from it, where the kidneys stop working properly. This is called haemolytic uraemic syndrome (HUS).

Bring your child to your GP if:

- they have diarrhoea that is not settling
- they have bloody diarrhoea
- you are concerned they might have VTEC

VTEC is very infectious. This is why children with VTEC are not allowed to attend crèches or other childminding facilities until they are free of infection.

Children in mainstream schools should not return to school until 48 hours have passed since their last episode of diarrhoea.

If your child has additional needs, your local HSE department of public health will advise you about when your child can return to school. Go to the HSE's Health Protection Surveillance Centre website at hpsc.ie for more information on VTEC.

Constipation

Constipation is when your child has a hard poo or does not go for a poo regularly. It is common.

Most children will do a poo once a day or every second day. Your child could be constipated if their poo is hard and painful to pass.

Other symptoms include crampy stomach pain, reduced appetite, small amounts of hard poo that look like rabbit droppings and soiled underwear.

What to do

Get your child to sit on the toilet after meals, even if they don't want to go.

Add foods high in fibre to your child's diet, like fruit, vegetables and wholegrain breads and cereals. Offer them lots of water to drink.

Encourage your child to be active (see page 24).

Talk to them to see if anything is worrying them.

Encourage them by praising them for things like sitting on the toilet, pooing in the toilet and washing their hands.

When to get medical help

Bring your child to see your GP or public health nurse if you think they have constipation, especially if making small changes to their diet and drinking doesn't help.

Your GP may prescribe a safe laxative for your child to take.

Chickenpox

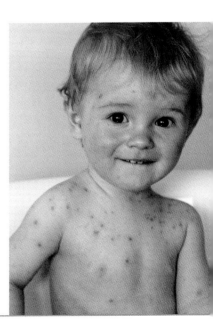

Chickenpox is caused by the varicella zoster virus. Your child can catch it by coming into contact with someone who has chickenpox.

If your child has not had chickenpox before, they can catch chickenpox from someone with shingles (an infection caused by the same virus). However, it's not possible to catch shingles.

The most obvious symptom is a red rash that can cover your child's entire body. Before the rash appears, your child may have a fever and some mild flu-like symptoms. These can include feeling unwell, a runny nose and aches and pains.

Chickenpox spots

Soon after the flu-like symptoms, an itchy rash appears. Some children may only have a few spots, but others are covered from head to toe.

Unusual symptoms

Most healthy children recover from chickenpox with no lasting ill-effects. But some are unlucky and have a more severe illness than usual.

Contact your GP straight away if they have any of the symptoms listed on page 55.

If your child gets a more severe dose of chickenpox, they may need to take prescription medicine. They may even need to go to hospital for treatment.

> **How chickenpox spreads**
>
> It is very easy for your child to catch chickenpox if they have not had it before.
>
> Chickenpox is spread by:
>
> - being in the same room as someone who has it
> - touching clothes or bedding that has fluid from chickenpox blisters on it
>
> Chickenpox is most infectious from one to two days before the rash appears until the blisters have all crusted over. This means that a child could be spreading chickenpox before anyone knows that they have it.
>
> It can take between 10 to 21 days after coming into contact with chickenpox for symptoms to appear.

How to help your child

The virus usually clears up by itself without any treatment. There are things you can do to ease your child's itching and discomfort. You can also take steps to stop chickenpox spreading.

Fever and pain

Give your child liquid paracetamol. It will help to relieve any pain and may help to control their temperature.

> Do not give your child ibuprofen if they have chickenpox. Research has found that serious skin reactions are more common in children with chickenpox who have been given ibuprofen.

Keep your child hydrated

It is important to encourage your child to drink. Sugar-free ice-lollies are a good way of getting fluids into children. They also help to soothe a sore mouth that has chickenpox spots in it. Avoid any food that may make your child's mouth sore, such as salty foods.

Stop the scratching

Chickenpox can be incredibly itchy, but it's important not to scratch the spots so as to avoid future scarring. Things that might help include:

✔ Getting a soothing cream or gel from your local pharmacy. This may help the itch and cool your child's skin.

✔ Asking your pharmacist if medication for the itch (known as antihistamines) might help. A sedating antihistamine may help your child to sleep at night.

✔ Dressing your child in comfy clothes. If they get too hot it might make their itch worse.

✔ Bathing your child in lukewarm water – a hot bath can make the itch worse.

✔ Patting their skin dry after a bath, don't rub.

✔ Keeping your child's fingernails clean and short. You can also put socks over your child's hands at night to stop them scratching the rash as they sleep.

> Your child will need to stay away from school or childcare until all the spots have crusted over. This is usually six days after the spots first appeared. It is a good idea to let your child's school, crèche or childminder know that your child has chickenpox, so they can alert other parents.

Complications

Some children are at risk of complications from chickenpox. This is a particular danger to children in high risk groups.

These children include:

- babies under the age of one month
- children with serious health problems such as heart and lung disease
- children on medications that affect their immune system such as chemotherapy

Contact your GP if your child has any of these issues and you think they have been exposed to chickenpox.

When to get medical help

Call your GP urgently if your child has chickenpox and:

- gets redness, pain and heat in the skin around a blister or spot
- they start to get pain in their chest or have difficulty breathing
- gets symptoms and signs of dehydration
- skin conditions like eczema
- headaches that don't go away after taking paracetamol or are getting worse
- is very unwell and you are concerned
- is in any of the high risk groups mentioned earlier on this page

Call your nearest hospital emergency department that treats children if your child has chickenpox and:

- is wobbly on their feet or suffers weakness
- is hard to wake or unusually drowsy
- is getting worse and becoming more unwell

Ring 999 or 112 if your child has chickenpox and they have a fit (also known as a seizure or a convulsion).

Ring ahead if you are bringing your child with chickenpox to the GP or hospital. They can take steps to reduce the risk of chickenpox spreading to vulnerable patients, for example, newborn babies.

Call your GP if you are pregnant and have been exposed to chickenpox, especially if you know you are not immune or if you are not sure.

Hand, foot and mouth disease

Hand, foot and mouth disease causes blisters on the hands and feet and in the mouth. Some children also have a sore throat and high temperature. These symptoms last for seven to 10 days.

Did you know?

Hand, foot and mouth disease is not the same as foot and mouth disease, which affects cattle, sheep and pigs. The two infections are unrelated, and you cannot catch hand, foot and mouth disease from animals.

How it spreads

The virus is spread by coughs and sneezes, and is also found in the poo of infected children. Some children infected with the virus do not have symptoms but can still pass it on to others. Symptoms start three to five days after becoming infected with the virus.

How to help your child

There is no specific treatment for hand, foot and mouth disease – it is usually a mild illness that goes away of its own accord. If a child feels unwell, liquid paracetamol may help. Always read the label. Keep medicine out of sight and reach of your children.

Make sure your child drinks plenty of fluids.

How to prevent it spreading

Since the virus is found in poo, make sure you wash your hands very carefully, especially before preparing food or after changing your child's nappy or helping your child use the potty or toilet. The virus can stay in the poo for many weeks after your child has recovered.

When to get help

Contact your GP if you are concerned or if your child has any of the symptoms listed on pages 47 to 48.

Hand, foot and mouth disease

Meningitis and septicaemia

Meningitis is an inflammation of the lining of the brain and spinal cord. There are two main types of meningitis: bacterial and viral. Septicaemia is a blood poisoning caused by bacteria.

Symptoms

Children with meningitis or septicaemia won't usually have every symptom.

They might not have a rash. Symptoms can appear in any order.

> Trust your instincts. A rash can often be a late sign. Don't wait for a rash.

Get medical help immediately if you think your child may have meningitis, or if they have some of the following symptoms:

Has a high temperature

- has a temperature of 38° or higher
- has cold hands and feet and is shivering

Dislikes bright lights

- squints or covers their eyes when exposed to light

Headache and neck stiffness

- has a headache
- has a stiff neck

Pain or body stiffness

- has aches or pains
- has joint or muscle pain
- has a stiff body, with jerking movements, or a floppy lifeless body

Tummy symptoms

- is vomiting or refusing to feed
- has stomach pain

Confused, tired or irritable

- is very sleepy, lethargic, not responding to you or difficult to wake
- is irritable when you pick them up
- has a high-pitched or moaning cry
- is confused or delirious

Skin colour

- has pale or bluish skin

A rash
- a rash that doesn't fade when you press a glass tumbler against it (see below)

Unusual breathing
- is breathing fast or is breathless

Seizures
- has seizures

> Not every child has all these symptoms at the one time. Septicaemia can occur with or without meningitis.

The glass tumbler test

How to check a rash

A rash does not always happen with meningitis. But it is important to check all of your child's body for a rash.

Look for tiny red or brown pin-prick marks that do not fade when a glass is pressed to the skin.

These marks can later change into larger red or purple blotches and into blood blisters.

The rash can be harder to see on darker skin, so check on the palms of the hands or the soles of the feet.

Do the glass tumbler test

1. Press the bottom or side of a clear drinking glass firmly against the rash.
2. Check if the rash fades under the pressure of the glass.
3. If the rash does not fade, your child may have septicaemia caused by the meningitis germ.
4. Get medical help at once.

Photo: Meningitis Research Foundation

Getting medical help

If you think your child is seriously ill, call 999 or 112 or bring your child immediately to the nearest emergency department.

If you're not sure, contact your GP or GP out of hours service immediately and ask for an urgent appointment.

Bring your child immediately to your nearest hospital emergency department for children if:

- you are unable to contact your GP
- they are unable to see your child urgently

Trust your instincts. If you think your child is ill, get medical help at once.

For more information on meningitis, see the Meningitis Research Foundation's website meningitis.org or locall 1890 41 33 44.

Giving medicine to young children

Never give a medicine to a child without first talking to your pharmacist, GP or public health nurse.

No aspirin

Don't give aspirin to children under 16, unless a GP prescribes it. There is a risk of serious illness.

Paracetamol

Make sure you have the right strength for your child. Check the correct dose on the label. It is dangerous to take too much paracetamol. Ask your pharmacist for advice and read all labels carefully.

Ibuprofen

You can give ibuprofen for pain and fever to children of three months and over who weigh more than 5kg (11lbs). Check the correct dose for your child's age.

Do not give ibuprofen to your child if they have chickenpox.

Ibuprofen may not be suitable for some children with asthma. Talk to your GP or pharmacist if in doubt.

> **Spoons and instructions**
>
> Always use the spoon or dosage syringe that comes with the medicine.
>
> Don't use household spoons. They come in different sizes and will not give your child the correct amount of medicine.
>
> Follow the dosage instructions very carefully. Give liquid medicines slowly to avoid choking.

Prevent poisoning

Keep medicines in their original containers. Keep all medicines, vitamins and food supplements out of the reach and sight of children and make sure lids are tightly closed.

Don't refer to medicine or vitamin tablets as sweets as children may be tempted to find them to take more.

Try not to take your own medication in front of your children because children love to copy what grown-ups do.

> Contact the Poisons Information Helpline on 01 809 2166 if you think that your child has taken medicine (or any poison). The helpline is open from 8am to 10pm every day. Outside of these hours, contact your GP or hospital. In an emergency call 999 or 112.

Preparing your child for hospital

Your child may have to stay in hospital at some stage, either after an emergency or for a planned operation or medical treatment.

How to prepare your child

- Children up to the age of 5 should be told about their hospital admission one to two days before it happens.
- Use dolls and teddies to play doctors and nurses with your child.
- Talk about hospitals as places where people go to get help to feel better.
- Reassure your child that you, or someone else that they love and trust, will be with them as much as possible.
- Tell them they will be coming home again.
- If the hospital policy allows, pack your child's favourite toy or blanket to soothe and comfort them.
- Read a book with pictures to your child about being in hospital.

> There are a number of stories you can read with your child to prepare them for their hospital stay, such as 'Neddy the Nebuliser', 'Lulu goes to hospital' and 'Goodbye tonsils'. For these and more, go to tallaghthospital.ie

In hospital

Explain as much as you can to your child so they know what is happening to them. Cuddle and reassure them as much as you can.

Be truthful. If something is going to hurt them, tell them. Otherwise your child may get distressed because it did hurt and they may not believe you the next time you tell them something.

Don't blame the nurse or doctor when something hurts. It is important that your child builds up a good relationship with them. Try not to make promises you can't keep such as "you only need to take this medicine once."

Your child's growth and development

Children develop at their own pace. Your support will help your child through this time of growth and development.

This section is a guide to the milestones that your child will achieve as they develop. The ages given are averages, and it is normal for children to gain one skill earlier than another.

What is important is how your child is developing overall. Try not to worry too much about the exact age at which certain milestones occur. For each milestone, there is a wide range of ages when children may reach it.

> If you are worried about how your child is developing overall, talk to your GP or public health nurse.

Posture and movement

2 to 3 years
Your child may:

- walk up and down stairs with help
- bend over and squat easily without falling
- stand on one foot for one to two seconds with help
- kick a ball forward
- begin to walk on the tips of their toes
- begin to pedal their tricycle
- turn a rotating handle on a door to open it
- build towers of nine to 10 blocks using both hands — but start to use one hand more often than the other
- turn the pages of a book one at a time
- pick up and thread large beads on a piece of string (with adult supervision)
- match colours, such as putting red with red and yellow with yellow

3 to 5 years

Your child may:

- walk up and down the stairs one foot for each step without help
- walk heel-to-toe
- walk around corners
- walk along a straight line drawn on the ground
- move forward and backward easily and quickly
- throw a ball from shoulder level
- catch a large bouncing ball most of the time
- begin to hold a crayon with their thumb and finger instead of their fist
- draw a person with three to four body parts such as a head, arms, body
- roll, pound, squeeze and pull modelling clay using their hands
- know the difference between many colours

4 to 5 years

Your child may:

- jump forward several times without falling
- stand on one foot for 10 seconds or more
- hop and turn cartwheels
- be able to skip
- copy triangles and other shapes
- draw a person with a full body
- write some capital letters
- thread beads on to a string easily (with adult supervision)
- drive pegs and shapes into holes
- draw crosses and circles easily
- cut a straight line on paper with safety scissors

Growth

Measuring your child's growth is one way of checking their overall health and development. Normal growth is more likely if your child has a healthy balanced diet and is emotionally secure. Other things such as genes, health and sickness can affect how your child grows.

Growth measurements

As your child grows, your public health nurse, GP and school nurse will monitor their growth. These checks include your child's weight and height. The results of these growth checks are recorded on your child's growth chart.

Growth charts

Growth charts show the pattern of growth healthy children usually follow. There are different charts for boys and girls because they usually have slightly different growth patterns.

When you look at a growth chart, you may notice that it has curved lines. These lines are called centiles. These show the average weight and height gain for children of different ages. The growth of your child will usually roughly follow a centile line.

Average weight gain

On average, a child gains 2 to 3kgs (4.5 to 6.5 lbs) each year until they reach puberty. But your child may gain more or less weight than this.

Average growth in height

On average, a child will grow between 4 to 6cm (1.5 to 2.5 inches) each year until puberty, but it's possible your child will grow more or less than this.

If they appear to be growing and developing normally, then weighing and measuring them twice a year is enough.

BMI (body mass index)

If your child is over the age of two, your GP or public health nurse may record their body mass index or BMI.

The BMI reading compares your child's weight to their height. BMI can be a better indicator of possible weight issues than just weight alone. If you are worried about your child's weight, ask your GP or health nurse to measure their BMI.

If you are concerned about your child's growth

Your public health nurse and GP will work closely with you to monitor your child's growth. If there are any concerns about your child's growth, they might be measured more often for a while.

Sometimes they might be referred to a specialist for further checks. This could be a HSE community medical doctor, HSE community dietitian or a paediatrician (a doctor who specialises in treating children).

Teeth

Your child should have most of their 20 baby teeth by the time they are two and a half years old. They will be 12 years old or more before the last baby tooth falls out.

At around five to six years of age, your child's baby teeth will begin to fall out and be replaced by permanent teeth. The front baby teeth, at the bottom of the mouth, are usually the first to fall out.

At around the same time, the first adult back teeth (molars) start to come through the gum right at the back of the mouth.

Because no baby teeth will fall out to make way for these new back teeth, it is very important to look out for signs of these new molar teeth to make sure they are cleaned properly.

Thumb-sucking and soothers

Some children continue to suck their thumb or a soother until they are four years old or even older. Your child may still be sucking their thumb or soother because it helps them cope with emotional issues. Issues can include a new baby in the family, going into hospital or starting preschool.

For some children, the attachment to sucking their thumb or soother is very strong. Don't try to stop them sucking if they are going through a stressful time.

Try not to criticise your children about sucking their thumb or soother. It could make them feel bad. Talk to your child, using language that is suitable for their age, about any stress or worries they might have. Show them that you care and that you understand.

Sucking their thumb or soother can affect tooth and jaw development in the long run. Your child may not have enough time to practice using their lips and tongue for talking or may not want to talk. This may take some time to correct. So, at some point, you will need to encourage your child to do something else instead.

Your child may also breathe through their mouth if sucking a soother, which can lead to too much dribbling.

What to do

If your child sucks their thumb

- Give them something else to do with their hands when they are playing or relaxing. They will be less likely to suck their thumb.
- Make sure their hands are clean so they don't get an infection in their mouth.
- Give them encouragement and praise for small successes when they try to stop thumb sucking.

If your child uses a soother

- Only use soothers at set times such as bedtime. Remove the soother when the child is asleep.
- Take your child's soother out when they are trying to talk or busy playing.
- Give rewards (not food). For older children, try using a star chart to praise them.
- Don't replace lost soothers.
- Give the soother to Santa, the Tooth Fairy or the Easter Bunny.
- Once your child has given up the soother, don't be tempted to give it back. Stick with it – they will forget about it in time.

See page 35 for information on caring for your child's teeth. Ask your dentist, public health nurse, GP or GP practice nurse for more advice.

Eyes

Your child's eyes will be checked between 21 and 24 months and again between three and four years old.

At these checks you will be asked if you have any concerns about how well your child can see. If there is a problem, your public health nurse may refer you for specialist treatment.

In junior infants class at primary school, a school public health nurse or your local public health nurse will check your child's eyes. At this check the nurse:

- notes any concerns you wrote on the consent form that you have to sign
- checks your child's vision using a special chart with letters

Some children already wear glasses when they go to school. They are included in the vision screening programme by being checked with their glasses on.

If you are concerned about your child's eyes

Many eye conditions are treatable if they are identified early. Contact your GP, public health nurse or the public health nurse who visits your child's school if you:

- notice something wrong with the appearance of your child's eyes or with their vision
- are concerned because a close family member, like a parent or sibling, has a lazy eye or squint (see next page)

If there is a problem, they may refer you to a HSE community medical doctor or a specialist community medical eye service.

Eye problems

Eye problems include:

Amblyopia

Amblyopia is also called lazy eye. It is poor vision in one or both eyes where normal eyesight did not develop during early childhood.

Squint

Squint is also called a cast or a turn. It means one eye looks in a different direction from the other. There are different types of squint. One or both eyes can appear to be:

- turning in (convergent)
- turning out (divergent)
- turning upward (vertically displaced)

You might notice that your child has a squint all the time, or it might be on and off. Children do not "grow out" of a true squint. It's important not to ignore squints. This is because squints can cause problems like:

- blurred vision
- double vision
- amblyopia or a "lazy eye" where your child doesn't develop normal eyesight

Squints can also cause your child to feel embarrassed and self-conscious.

Hearing

In junior infants class at primary school, a school public health nurse or your local public health nurse will check your child's hearing.

At this check, the nurse:

- notes any concerns you wrote on the consent form that you have to sign
- uses a small screening audiometer with headphones to test if your child can hear high and low pitched noises

How your child's hearing develops

2 years to 5 years

Your child should:

- understand differences in meaning ("go-stop", "in-on", "up-down")
- follow two requests ("get the book and put it on the table")

3 to 4 years

Your child should:

- hear you when you call from another room
- answer simple "who?", "what?", "where?", and "why?" questions

4 to 5 years

Your child should:

- pay attention to a short story and answer simple questions about what happened
- hear and understand most of what is said at home and at school

---

If you are concerned about your child's hearing

As a parent, you are best placed to know if your child is hearing well for their age. You will know by how your child listens, talks and behaves compared to other children their age. If you are concerned about your child's hearing, contact either:

- the school public health nurse or your local public health nurse
- your GP or practice nurse

Your child may be referred to the HSE community medical doctor or local children's audiology services.

You can contact these services during your child's preschool years and when your child is in primary school.

Childhood speech, language and hearing checklist

2 to 3 years

What your child should be able to do:

Hearing and understanding	Talking
• Understands differences in meaning ("go-stop", "in-on", "big-little", "up-down"). • Follows 2 requests ("Get the book and put it on the table"). • Listens to and enjoys hearing stories for longer periods of time.	• Has a word for almost everything. • Uses two or three words to talk about and ask for things. • Uses k, g, f, t, d, and n sounds. • Speech is understood by familiar listeners most of the time. • Often asks for or directs attention to objects by naming them.

3 to 4 years

What your child should be able to do:

Hearing and understanding	Talking
• Hears you when you call from another room. • Hears television or radio at the same loudness level as other family members. • Answers simple "who?", "what?", "where?", and "why?" questions.	• Talks about activities at school or at friends' homes. • People outside of the family usually understand child's speech. • Uses a lot of sentences that have 4 or more words. • Usually talks easily without repeating syllables or words.

4 to 5 years

What your child should be able to do:

Hearing and understanding	Talking
• Pays attention to a short story and answers simple questions about them. • Hears and understands most of what is said at home and in school.	• Uses sentences that give lots of details ("The biggest peach is mine"). • Tells stories that stick to topic. • Communicates easily with other children and adults. • Says most sounds correctly except a few like l, s, r, v, z, ch, sh, th. • Says rhyming words. • Names some letters and numbers. • Uses the same grammar as the rest of the family.

Text reproduced with permission from "How Does Your Child Hear and Talk." Available from http://www.asha.org/public/speech/development/chart.htm.

Talk to your GP or public health nurse if you are concerned about your child's speech, language or hearing.

Speech and language development

Each child develops speech and language skills at their own pace. Be patient with your child as their speech develops. You will find that helping and encouraging them is a very rewarding experience for you both that also helps to build on the loving relationship between you.

The information here is offered as a guide only because all children develop at different rates. If you are concerned or would like more information or support, please contact your public health nurse or GP. They may refer you to your local HSE speech and language therapy service.

Your child's language communication development

2 to 3 years

This is a really exciting time for your child's language and communication development.

Their understanding of words and phrases is growing quickly. They are beginning to:

- understand short questions or instructions. For example: "Where's granddad's car?" or: "Find the small cup"
- understand different types of words. For example action words (running, eating), describing words (big, soft), location words (on, in) and pronouns (he, she, I)
- understand simple "who", "what", and "where" questions
- listen to short and simple stories

Your child will begin to use short sentences to express their needs, thoughts and ideas. You will notice your child:

- using from 50 to 300 words – their vocabulary is quickly expanding
- starting to express short sentences of two to five words. For example: "more cheese" or "me want more cheese"
- missing out some words or using immature words. For example: "daddy eating" for "daddy is eating" or "me falled over" for "I fell over"
- asking questions. For example: "What's that?"
- talking a lot during imaginative play, for example when feeding their doll or driving a car
- recognising and naming their own and other people's feelings. For example: "Mammy, I'm happy"
- developing clearer speech sounds, but some pronunciations will still sound immature. For example: "boon" instead of "spoon" or "tup" instead of "cup"
- talking about events that have already happened

3 to 5 years

At this stage your child is enjoying full conversations. They are using their language to talk to family and friends or work out problems. A massive amount of learning is happening at this time.

As your child's understanding continues to develop, you will notice how they:

- understand longer instructions. For example: "Get your shoes and come outside"
- listen to stories and answer questions about what they've heard such as, "Who did the bear see?"
- understand words about colours and numbers – "give me two red blocks"
- understand and enjoy simple jokes

- understand "why" and "how" questions (by four and a half years)
- begin to understand time concepts. For example: "We are going to Nana's tomorrow"

As your child takes part in more conversations you will notice them:

- using longer sentences with well-developed grammar. For example: "I went to the park and I played on the swings"
- using words that join sentences together ("and", "because", "if")
- asking lots of questions like "how?" and "why?"
- answering questions about why something has happened
- telling a short story in sequence. For example: "We went to the beach, I built a sandcastle and then we jumped into the water"
- showing interest in learning new words and asking what new words mean
- using language to engage in imaginative play, negotiate with others and have longer conversations
- developing clear speech. By the age of four years, most children will have developed all sounds apart from "ch", "j", "r". By the age of five, most children will have developed all sounds apart from "r"

How you can support your child's communication

Your relationship and interactions with your child are what's most important in helping their speech, language and communication to develop.

You can support your child's communication by:

- Talking to them about everyday activities and routines. For example: "After we visit Granny, we will go to the shops."
- Starting with a comment instead of a question. A comment invites your child to answer with more than just 'yes' or 'no'. For example, instead of asking, "Is that a sand castle?" say, "I see you are building a lovely sand castle. Tell me about it."
- Having 10 minutes "special time" in which you play at an activity that your child has chosen.
- Modelling correct grammar or pronunciation. For example, if your child makes a mistake – say, "Oh yes, the boy fell off the wall" if your child says, "the boy falled off the wall".

- Repeating your child's sentences and adding extra words or new ideas. For example, if your child says; "Look at the tiger", you could say: "Oh wow, look at the stripy tiger. I wonder what he likes to eat."
- Making up stories together – you can think up new and interesting characters and places.
- Playing word games or sound games. For example, words that start with b; words that rhyme with cat or word-meaning games. For example: "name five animals".
- Playing games like 'Simon says' to help your child to understand and follow simple instructions.
- Reading books together then talking about the story and what you think might happen next.
- Trying to limit screen time to one hour each day. Screen time can take away from special interactions with your child that are important for speech and language development. See page 106.

See page 65 for tips to help stop soother use. Soothers can lead to difficulties with your child's teeth and speech development.

If your child repeats sounds or words

Because your child's language is developing so quickly at this time, it is very common to hear them repeating sounds in words or whole words. For example: "m-m-m-m-mammy can I have juice" or "I-I-I-I-I-I want that."

You can help them by:

- listening to what they have said and not how they have said it
- keeping eye contact and letting them know that they have lots of time to finish what they are saying
- speaking slowly with your child and asking fewer questions
- reducing distractions, for example turn off the TV and radio and put down your phone

Most children pass through this phase with ease.

Possible signs your child may not be developing as expected

The list below is only a guide to possible problems with your child's development. If you are concerned that your child is not developing, contact your public health nurse or GP. They can study your child's behaviour and development.

They also provide you and your family with support, developmental guidance and referrals if you need them.

Things you should look out for

2 years

- cannot use toys for their purpose, for example they are banging blocks together rather than using them to build
- is not learning new words
- cannot put words together like "push swing"
- is making no attempts to feed themselves using a spoon
- is not helping you get them dressed, for example not holding up their arms when you are putting on their vest
- cannot walk independently
- cannot go up the stairs while holding onto your hand or the bannister

3 years

- falls a lot and has difficulty climbing stairs
- is constantly drooling or has very unclear speech
- does not get involved in pretend play
- does not understand simple instructions
- cannot copy a circle
- has little interest in other children
- has extreme difficulty separating from you
- makes poor eye contact with you and others
- has very limited interest in toys
- cannot build a tower of more than four blocks
- has no interest in being toilet trained or dressing themselves

4 years

- cannot throw a ball from shoulder level
- cannot ride a tricycle
- cannot grasp a crayon between their thumb and fingers
- has difficulty scribbling
- cannot stack 4 blocks
- doesn't use sentences of more than 3 words
- doesn't use 'me' and 'you' correctly
- still clings or cries when you leave them or their carer leaves
- shows no interest in games with others
- doesn't respond to people outside the family
- doesn't engage in pretend play
- cannot copy a circle
- lashes out without any self-control when they are angry or upset

5 years

- acts very fearfully or timidly, or aggressively
- is unable to separate from you without a major protest
- is easily distracted and unable to concentrate on any single activity for more than 5 minutes
- shows little interest in playing with other children
- seems unhappy or sad much of the time
- has trouble eating, sleeping or using the toilet
- cannot understand a two-part command such as "put the doll in the bed and cover it with blankets"
- cannot correctly give their first and last name
- doesn't talk about their daily activities
- cannot build a tower of 6 to 8 blocks
- has trouble taking off their clothes
- cannot wash and dry their hands

Caring for your child with special needs

If your child has special needs or a long-term illness, this can bring extra adjustments to your family's life. As a parent, you may have difficult feelings to cope with. You may also have to make extra decisions for your child and your family.

Your GP and public health nurse are there to help. They can offer information and support to guide you. They can also refer you to other services that you may need.

Useful websites

When your child is diagnosed with a particular condition, you may look for information online. You should always remember that, while the internet is a great source of information, a lot of that information may be out of date, unreliable or incorrect.

Also, the information you find online may not be relevant to your child's own needs, even if it is about the same condition. Each child is different.

If you have recently found out about your child's disability or developmental delay, one site you may find helpful is: informingfamilies.ie

Although everyone's experience is different, it might help you to speak to other parents who have children with needs similar to your child's. They are likely to have been through the same emotions and pathways. They may be able to offer you some practical advice.

The Special Needs Parents Association is run by parents. Their aim is to provide support and information to the families of children with a disability or special needs. See specialneedsparents.ie

You can find out about services for children with disabilities at hse.ie/childdisability. This also has a list of websites which have useful information about some childhood conditions.

Services for children with special needs

If your child is diagnosed with a disability or there are concerns that their development may be delayed, it is important that you get support so you can provide the extra care your child needs to reach their potential.

Your child may need services such as physiotherapy or speech and language therapy. Parents can find out about how to encourage their child's development and get advice on practical issues. What services you and your child are offered depends on the needs of your child.

Health services for children with a disability or developmental delay are provided either by the HSE itself or by certain voluntary organisations which are funded by the HSE.

Many children with delays in their development can have their needs met by their local HSE Primary Care services such as a community speech and language therapist or physiotherapist.

Children's disability teams provide services for children with complex needs, which are best met through the support of a team of professionals working closely together.

Children's disability services vary across the country. You can see a list of the services in your area at hse.ie/childdisability or talk to your public health nurse about what's available near you and how to refer your child.

Financial entitlements

Information on benefits and entitlements is available on citizensinformation.ie

Domiciliary care allowance

This is a monthly payment made to the carer of a child with a severe disability who lives at home. See welfare.ie

Carer's benefit

This is a payment made to people who leave the workforce to care for a person or people who need full-time care and attention. See welfare.ie

Carer's allowance

This is a payment to people on low incomes who are looking after a person who needs support because of age, disability or illness. See welfare.ie

Carer's support grant

This is an annual grant made to carers. It is paid automatically to people getting carer's allowance (full-rate or half-rate), carer's benefit or domiciliary care allowance. See welfare.ie

Long term illness scheme

This includes free drugs, medicines and medical and surgical appliances for the treatment of certain conditions. The scheme does not depend on your income or other circumstances. See hse.ie

Medical card for people receiving domiciliary care allowance

If you are getting domiciliary care allowance to care for your child, they are eligible for a medical card without a means test. See hse.ie

Incapacitated child tax credit

This is a tax credit which you can claim if you have a child who is permanently incapacitated. See revenue.ie

Housing grants for adapting your home

Grants may be available to help you adapt your home so it can be used by a person with a physical, sensory or intellectual disability or a mental health difficulty. Contact your local city or county council for details.

'Better Energy Warmer Homes' scheme

Funds are available to make the homes of families receiving the domiciliary care allowance warmer and more energy efficient. See seai.ie

Tax reliefs for drivers and passengers with disabilities

There is a range of tax reliefs to help reduce the cost of buying and using a vehicle which has been specially constructed or adapted for a driver or passenger with a disability. See revenue.ie

Equipment

Depending on their particular needs and difficulties, your child might benefit from equipment such as a walking aid or a special seat.

A health professional such as an occupational therapist can help you find out what equipment is available to help your child and how you can apply for it to be supplied or funded.

If you have a medical card or long term illness card, the HSE may provide equipment which has been prescribed by a health professional. If you have private health insurance, it might cover funding for some equipment, so check with your insurer.

Preschool supports

The Access and Inclusion Model (AIM) supports children with disabilities so that they can access and fully participate in their local preschool.

If your child needs support to attend, including equipment or expert advice from an early years specialist, the preschool will make an application with your help and permission to AIM.

See aim.gov.ie for more information and talk to your preschool provider.

Choosing a school for your child

Deciding where any child is to be educated can be a big decision but can be of even greater concern to parents of children with special educational needs.

The majority of children with special educational needs now attend their local primary or post-primary mainstream school. Some children may benefit from the support of a special school, for part or all of their education.

The National Council for Special Education has booklets with information and advice for parents of children with special educational needs. See ncse.ie

Home supports

Caring for a child with special needs, especially if they have complex medical needs, can put a lot of extra pressure on parents and carers.

Home support is when a family support worker takes over care of your child for a period of time to allow parents some time off. The availability of this service varies across the country, so talk to your public health nurse or your child's disability team to find out if it is available.

Assessing your child's needs

Your child is entitled to an 'assessment of need' under the Disability Act if you think that they have a disability.

You can contact an assessment officer through your local HSE health centre. See hse.ie

Please note that it is not essential to go through the assessment of need process to access services for your child. They can be referred directly.

See hse.ie/progressingdisabilityservices for more information.

Your child's social, emotional and behavioural development

Just as when they were a baby, the relationship between you and your child between the ages of two and five provides the foundation for their good health and well-being throughout the rest of their life.

By having a secure relationship with you, your child will:

- feel more confident exploring their environment
- learn about and understand various feelings
- begin to form new relationships
- be encouraged to become more independent, knowing as they explore that they can return again to the safety of your presence

The stage between ages two and five is a time of great change for your child. They will develop socially and emotionally during this time. You will need to adapt your parenting skills to correspond to your child's stage of development.

Testing boundaries

As your child gains independence and confidence, challenging behaviours can occasionally arise. It is normal for children of this age to test boundaries. These behaviours can be difficult for parents to understand. The word "no" is commonly used during this stage of development.

Although your child is gaining independence, they still need your help to understand their big feelings as well as your support to follow rules and boundaries.

Every child develops at their own pace. The information here is a guide to help you understand and promote your child's development. There are also some tips about how to manage challenging behaviours that may become more common as your child learns how to express themselves.

Children's social, emotional and behavioural development is very important so that they can enjoy their lives and grow to be confident and secure.

2 to 3 years

Spend time playing with your child and observing their play. This will help you become familiar with their stage of development.

Ways to spend time with your child include:

- Talking to them about everyday events and things that you do.
- Allowing them to safely help you with some activities around the home.
- Enjoying the simple things in life together – like the flowers in the garden, the sensations as you mix and prepare food together.
- Reading with your child.

The time you spend with your child, sharing conversations and experiences, will help them feel safe and secure as they grow. Try to talk positively to and about your child, as children are very sensitive.

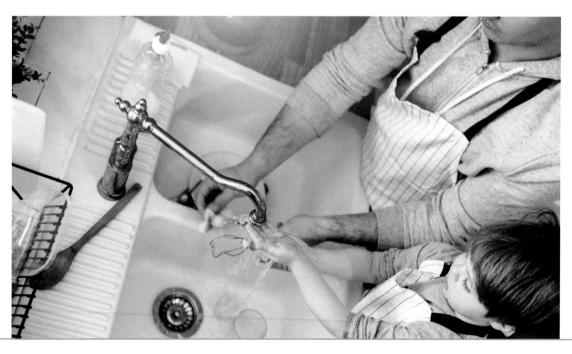

You may notice that your child:

- may ask questions all the time
- may be very interested in all parts of their body
- will often use the word "no" as they gain confidence
- will love sharing their achievements with you. They will love getting praise and encouragement from you.
- may appear to think the world revolves around them. This is because, for them, it does! Children of this age cannot put themselves in the shoes of others.
- will become interested in their peers and other adults. They may enjoy talking to them.
- has increasing confidence that means they will be able to manage being apart from you for short periods of time, for example going to preschool

3 to 4 years

As your child reaches the age of 3, their personality will begin to become more obvious to you.

Some children are naturally confident and are risk-takers while others are reserved and cautious. Some children manage big emotions well, others need more support and time to recover from big emotions. Some are strong-willed, others are more easy-going. Some are anxious, others are more relaxed.

The more time you spend with your child, the more you will understand their personality. This will help you identify their strengths as well as areas where support may be needed. Knowing your child's personality may also help you to choose positive strategies for managing challenging behaviour.

The way you view your child will have an impact on how they view themselves. The more positive that view is, the better your child's self-esteem will be. This means that your child's sense of self will be a positive one. Having a positive sense of self will improve your child's resilience when they are faced with challenges.

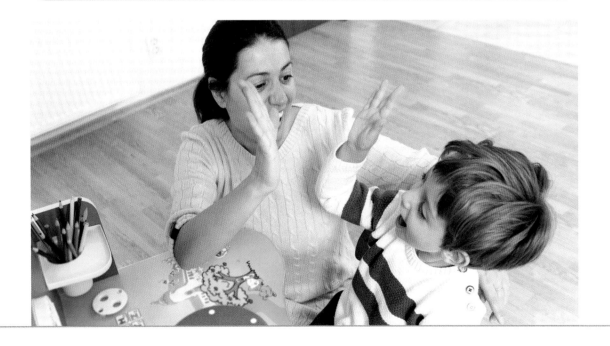

It is important to accept your child's personality as this is unlikely to change. Some personality traits are inherited from our parents, others are shaped by our world, our families and our cultures.

Try to avoid making negative comments on your child's behaviour and their emerging personality. Children are often very sensitive to these comments. They want and need your approval.

You may notice that your child will:

- play for longer periods of time – both independently and with other children
- have fewer tantrums
- be more able to follow directions
- be more able to accept limits that you set
- become more aware of their feelings
- still like to share all their achievements with you
- be able to participate in group activities
- be more able to follow the rules you set

But remember: despite this progress, they will still need your support and reminders. They will often enjoy when their good behaviour is rewarded.

4 to 5 years

It is lovely to watch your child's personality emerging. Try not to compare your child to other children. Focus on your child and how they have grown and developed over the past few years.

You may notice that your child:

- may still need your support when trying to talk to other adults
- will understand what you are saying. They will often repeat what they hear. This can be embarrassing for some parents
- may make comments about things they notice. They are still not aware that some comments can be hurtful. For example, you may be in a crowded lift with your child when they pipe up "Mammy, why is that man so fat?"
- may begin to show an interest in time
- may be interested in learning new and more complicated games
- may show their competitive streak when playing games
- will be better at taking turns and sharing but still needs encouragement from time to time
- may be more confident but will still rely on your support
- will be more aware of dangers such as road safety. They will still need your help to stay safe
- may behave as though the world revolves around them
- will enjoy showing off their achievements

Tips for encouraging social and emotional development

Having a secure relationship with you will help your child have the confidence to explore their world. They will feel secure knowing that they can return to you. Even the most ordinary everyday moments can help to shape your child's social and emotional development.

Show them affection

Show your child that you love them by giving them lots of physical affection, plenty of cuddles and kisses and telling them you love them.

Give time to your child

Make time to play, chat and listen to your child. This lets them know that they are important.

Encourage play

Children need to play on their own and with others to learn many life skills such as winning and losing, having fun and chatting to others.

Build their confidence, self-esteem and independence

Talk to and about your child in a positive way. Encourage positive behaviours with praise. For example, try saying "I love it when you play gently" instead of "you're always so rough".

Allow them, where possible, to make choices and decisions, for example: "Do you want to wear your blue coat or your yellow coat?" This can help avoid arguments about wearing a coat. Allow them and encourage them to be as independent as possible, for example when dressing or feeding themselves.

Encourage your child to experience new situations. This will help their confidence to grow.

> Remember that all children develop at their own pace. Encourage your child, but try not to force them to achieve milestones before they are ready.
>
> Learn to accept what your child can and cannot do. We all have strengths and weaknesses.

Respect your child

All children deserve to be treated with courtesy and dignity, just like adults. Your child learns respect from what you do.

For example, suppose you correct your child for misbehaviour. Later, you find out that you were wrong. You can show them the appropriate way to behave by saying that you were wrong and you are sorry.

Helping your child to manage their feelings

Your child's feelings are important, and helping your child to name or label their emotions helps them to express them. Try to encourage your child and show them positive ways to manage big feelings like worry, anger and frustration.

Be a role model. Your child will watch how you deal with certain feelings and may copy your behaviour.

Empathy is the ability to "walk in another person's shoes" or see the world from someone else's point of view.

Empathy starts to emerge between ages 2 to 3. This is when children begin to show empathic concern for other children around the same age. For example, becoming distressed by another child's distress.

Empathy develops gradually. It takes more time (around ages 4 to 5) for your child to think about the perspective of others.

You can encourage the development of empathy by helping your child to name their feelings and showing ways to positively deal with feelings.

Keep to a routine

Children feel secure if things happen at roughly the same time each day. If you need to change anything, explain why.

How to guide your child's behaviour

As your child develops and begins to show their independence, you may find the ages between 2 and 5 to be an exciting and rewarding time.

In some ways, your life may become easier as your child starts to do more things for themselves. But this can also be a challenging time for young children and for parents.

Your child begins to learn what they like and dislike. They do not have the language to express this, and do not know how to deal with big feelings. Sometimes this can result in behaviours that are difficult to manage, like tantrums, irrational demands and even aggressive behaviour.

As a parent you have an important job to do as you begin to teach your child about the types of behaviours that are acceptable for their age. How you respond to difficult behaviours will help your child to manage difficult situations in the future.

> Remember that your young child is not able to see the world from anyone else's point of view. Try not to react, even though this is hard. Encourage positive behaviour by setting clear rules and boundaries. Give your child lots of positive attention when they behave well.

Children thrive in a loving, low-conflict, safe and predictable environment. Allow your child the opportunity to be more independent and to make decisions for themselves. Although they may make mistakes, this is part of learning.

> ## Dealing with your feelings if your child has difficult behaviours
>
> - 'Tune in' to how you are feeling yourself. Try not to react immediately. Take a moment to think about how to respond.
> - See your child's behaviour as a normal part of development. This is not the same as giving in to their every demand. But if you understand why they are reacting the way they are it is easier to respond with empathy.
> - You cannot force your child to behave in a certain way. The only thing you can directly control is how you respond to the situation. Feeling angry and frustrated is normal, but tuning in and seeing your child's point of view helps you not to react in anger.

Tips for encouraging positive behaviours

As a parent, you can support your child to:

- be confident
- get on well with their family and other children

- learn new skills and behaviours
- become more independent over time, solve problems and be able to do more things for themselves as they grow

The following tips can help:

Notice and praise good behaviour

No matter how small the good behaviour is, praise it as soon as you see it. Your child will love the attention, and repeat the behaviour so that they can get more attention.

Praise the specific behaviour you want to see more of. Say things like: "Thanks for tidying your toys away, I really like the way you put them in the basket." That way they will know what you are praising them for and will be more likely to repeat it.

Have clear rules and boundaries

They need to be short, easy to understand, fair and apply to everybody in the home.

Use positive instead of negative words – for example say "please sit down when you're eating" instead of "don't run around with food". Be consistent so children get to know these rules.

Model good behaviour

You are your child's role model and they are likely to copy what you do. So, if you act calmly and respectfully it can encourage your child to do the same.

Anticipate problems

If you know you are going to be waiting somewhere for a period of time, think of activities you and your child can do together to keep them occupied.

Problems are more likely to occur when your child is hungry or tired. Having healthy snacks to hand is often a good idea. Try not to plan activities during nap time or close to bedtime.

Keep to a routine

Children feel secure if things happen at roughly the same time each day. If you need to change anything, explain why.

Consistency

If you are co-parenting it's important to be aware that sometimes parents can have different styles. Try to be respectful of each other and compromise. It is less confusing for your child if you are both consistent with discipline.

> **Parenting programmes and courses**
>
> If you would like to know more about ways to encourage your child's positive behaviour, look out for parenting programmes in your area.
>
> These programmes deliver training to support parents by introducing a range of parenting strategies that can support positive behaviours and also help to manage misbehaviours. See page 15 for more information on parenting courses.

If your child misbehaves

Even a child who is well behaved most of the time will, from time to time, test boundaries and limits. It is important to think ahead to how you will manage this behaviour when it happens.

Stay as calm as you can and do not get upset or angry. Remember that this is all part of your child's normal growth and development. They are learning from your reaction to their misbehaviour. It is your choice as a parent to decide which strategies you use with your child.

Some tips include:

If the behaviour is minor

Ignore the behaviour if it is minor and your child or others are not being put at risk by it. Your child will realise they will not get attention for this behaviour and, generally, if they don't get attention for it, they will stop.

If minor misbehaviour continues

You need to act if minor misbehaviour continues. Try not to shout, as if you react calmly your child is more likely to react calmly in future. A firm explanation is usually more effective.

Act quickly, have a plan in place and be consistent. If you don't follow through with what you said would happen, children quickly learn from this and will be less likely to stop the misbehaviour.

Make it clear that it is the misbehaviour that is wrong and not your child. This is important as it may affect their self-esteem if you criticise them rather than what they have done. For example, instead of saying: "You are a naughty girl. Why can't you be good?" you could say: "Aoife, throwing food is not nice. Please eat your sandwich and don't throw food."

Plan ahead. It is always best to deal with issues like tiredness or hunger that might cause your child to be upset or misbehave. For example, if shopping time clashes with nap time, wait until after nap time to go shopping. If you go shopping with a child who is tired they may be more likely to misbehave.

If the misbehaviour is more serious and your child is over 3

1. Remove your child from where they are misbehaving.
2. Explain that this behaviour is not acceptable and why it is not acceptable.
3. Tell them that they can return to the activity when they calm down. Only allow your child to return to the activity when they have calmed down.

If the behaviour is particularly serious, you can discipline them. Over the next few pages, we suggest some of the strategies such as 'time out' that you can use.

Consequences that fit the misbehaviour

If children are fighting over a toy or activity, you can remove that toy or activity for a short period of time. Explain that you expect them to play nicely and you will only return the toy or activity when they calm down. When you return the toy or activity, explain the rules again. If the fighting happens again, take away the toy or activity for a longer period.

Reward charts

Reward charts can be helpful but they need to be specific if you want to target a particular behaviour problem. For example, if your child is hitting, look for two times during the day when they are not hitting anyone. Praise your child and put two stickers on the reward chart.

When your child has a certain amount of stickers, reward them with a treat like a trip to the park or a small toy. It is better if the treats are not food.

Time out

Time out is a way to take a child who is misbehaving out of a stressful situation for a short time. It gives you and your child a chance to calm down before re-joining others. It is important that they know that it is their misbehaviour that is being corrected and not them as a person.

Time out is not useful if your child:

- is under three years old and does not understand why they are being disciplined
- has special needs and is unable to co-operate with you in spending time alone

For time out to work, your child must be able to know:

- what they did wrong
- what they should have done instead
- that they will get a chance to behave as you expect them to. Once they behave the way you want them to they will get a chance to rejoin an activity

When to use time out

Time out should not be used as a punishment. It should be seen as a chance to take a break. Try not to use time out when you are angry. Rather, use it when your child is so out of control (kicking, throwing, biting) that they will not accept comfort from you. When that happens, you and your child will both benefit from taking a break.

Your child needs to be very clear about what behaviour will lead to time out. Some examples are hitting, biting or throwing things even after you ask them to stop.

You may wish to give your child a warning to change their behaviour before you use time out. If you do give a warning, make sure you follow through with time out if their unacceptable behaviour continues. It is important that everyone who cares for your child will stick to the small list of misbehaviours that your child knows will lead to time out.

Do not use time out for other minor misbehaviours in the heat of the moment.

Steps for successful time out

Create a safe space

Identify a safe quiet place for your child to sit where there are no distractions. Good places are a chair or beanbag by the wall or on the bottom step of the stairs. You can see your child and be near them. Talk to your child about what this space is for: "This is a place where we go to take a break and calm down."

Name the space

Giving the space a name can help, like 'calming corner'.

Guide your child to the space calmly

If your child behaves in an unacceptable way such as hurting someone or refusing to hold hands when crossing the road, then you simply tell them what has happened: "Sofia you have hurt your brother. That behaviour is not allowed. You need to go to the calming corner and when you have calmed down you can come back to play."

If they leave the space

If your child comes out of the time out area before their time is up and wants to re-join the play, place them back in the time out area, provided they will be safe there. After they have stayed calm for the period of time you intended, allow them to re-join the group.

How long to leave your child in time out

Time outs don't have to be long to be effective. A rough guide is one minute of time out for every year of age. For example, a four-year-old should be in time out for a maximum of four minutes. Use a timer as this will help your child to learn that when the time is up, you will check back in with them.

After the time out period

At the end of time out, do not start nagging your child about their previous misbehaviour. Simply try to return to positive attention. When you notice your child behaving well again, give them praise so that they can see this is the behaviour you like and want to see more of.

Alternatives to time out – 'time in' and planned ignoring

'Time in'

If your child is out of control but will accept soothing from you, physically comfort your child to help them calm down. For example, give them a hug. This is not giving in. This is helping your child to calm down so that the situation can be handled in a calm way.

Planned ignoring

If your child is out of control but not harming themselves or others, ignoring the behaviour can be helpful. Paying attention to something else, like a truck passing the home, can distract your child and help move them from the distressing situation.

When you are managing misbehaviour

✔ Stay calm.

✔ Be realistic in what you expect from your child (for example many small children cannot handle long shopping trips).

✔ Tell your child how you expect them to behave.

✔ Explain what is wrong when your child does misbehave.

✔ Set a good example.

✔ Use time out or alternatives.

✔ Remember your child is not doing this on purpose. Challenging behaviour is a normal part of their growth and development.

✔ Ask for help – it is normal to feel angry and frustrated at times.

✔ Ask for advice, especially if the behaviour continues and you feel lost.

✔ Look out for parenting programmes in your area. You could learn strategies to help you promote positive behaviour.

Tantrums

Tantrums are very common. A tantrum is your growing child's way of expressing their feelings.

During a tantrum, your child may do things like shout, scream, kick, bite, throw themselves to the floor or throw things about. Tantrums tend to become less frequent by the time your child reaches the age of 3.

Did you know?

Believe it or not, tantrums can be a positive thing. They are an opportunity to teach your child how to manage frustration and anger. Being able to deal with challenges and with big feelings like anger, and to express them in appropriate ways, are important life skills.

Not all children have tantrums, and for some they may only occur occasionally. For other children, tantrums are more frequent. It can be stressful for parents to see their child having a tantrum. Being in public adds an extra element of stress. You may feel embarrassed when your child has a tantrum in public. When you feel embarrassed, it is harder to remain calm.

There are some things you can do to help you to deal with tantrums when they happen.

Tips for managing tantrums

It can be very difficult to stay calm when your child is having a tantrum. You may not realise it, but even when they are having a tantrum your child is watching you to see how you react. When you stay calm you are modelling the behaviour you would like them to have. Your calmness will help your child to feel safe.

Some of the tips on page 90 may be helpful in addition to the tips below.

Think about why the tantrum is happening

By having a tantrum your child is expressing what they are feeling. Perhaps they are hungry or tired. Maybe they do not want to share a toy with another child. Perhaps they are feeling jealous.

Understanding why the tantrum is happening can help you to deal with it. After all, we all feel angry and frustrated at times. We just express it differently.

Prevention

You can sometimes help prevent tantrums if you avoid letting your child become too hungry or tired. Keep shopping trips short.

Saying "no"

When you say "no", say it firmly and calmly and offer your child another option. For example, encourage other good aspects of their behaviour, such as getting them to join in play with you and others. Remember, it is the tone of your voice and their understanding of the word "no" that is important to learn at an early age.

Be consistent

Don't change your mind just because your child is having a tantrum. If the tantrum has happened because you have said "no" to something, do not say "yes" no matter how tempted you may be. It might resolve this tantrum, but soon your child will realise that tantrums result in them getting what they want.

Wait it out

Sometimes there is nothing you can do except wait for the tantrum to pass. This can feel like a very long time, especially in public. Try not to feel embarrassed. Ignore other people who may be around, and focus on remaining calm. People with small children themselves are likely to be very sympathetic - it could be their child next!

Keep your child close

If possible, hug and reassure your child, talk out what you think may be going on in their head: "I know you're angry that you can't have sweets..."

Be sensitive to your child though. Some children will not want to be hugged or touched during a tantrum. Stay with your child to make sure they do not come to physical harm.

Reasoning with your child may not work

If your young child is too upset to listen to or understand what you are saying, they won't be open to logic.

Look after yourself

If you find yourself becoming angry or upset with your child's behaviour, see if you can get another adult to take over minding them while you take some time for yourself.

Biting, hitting, kicking and other unacceptable behaviours

Many young children occasionally bite, hit and kick others. This might include other children or even a parent. It is normal for young children to test limits. These behaviours can happen because your child needs to express a strong feeling such as anger.

It may also be their way of telling you they need more personal space. Sometimes they are simply experimenting to see what will happen or what kind of a reaction they will get.

As your child grows older they should learn that these behaviours will hurt others. It is important that you teach your child that these behaviours are not acceptable. With time you will notice the times when these behaviours are more likely to occur and you may be able to prevent them from happening.

Ways to prevent unacceptable behaviours

- Keep an eye on your child especially when they are around other children.
- Think about when these behaviours normally happen.
- If you see your child is about to bite, hit or kick, intervene to distract them. Show them an interesting book or toy.
- If you think your child bites, hits or kicks when they need personal space, keep an eye on the space around your child. "Jake, would you mind sitting over here so Anna has a bit of space?"
- Suggest ways to share and take turns. One strategy is to use an egg timer so children can see how long they have to play with the toy before sharing.

How to deal with unacceptable behaviours

Be aware of your own feelings

Count to 10 or take a few deep breaths before you respond. If an older child is hitting their newborn baby brother or sister it is normal for your protective instincts to make you want to react with anger. Try and react calmly and gently.

Firmly but calmly state that the behaviour is wrong

For example: "No biting. Biting hurts. Look Jake is crying now." Keep it short and simple. It is important to not give much attention to the behaviour.

Focus your attention on the child who was hurt

Show concern and sympathy to the child who has been hurt. By doing this, you are not giving attention to the child who has bitten, hit or kicked. Children love attention so by not giving them that attention, the unacceptable behaviour seems unrewarding. It also shows empathy for the child who was hurt.

If the other child tries to join in as you soothe the child who has been hurt, remind them to wait because their behaviour was unacceptable.

During playtime

Don't make the children play again together unless they want to.

It can help to think about activities that don't need children to share, like sand and water play. These may give them a chance to relax.

This takes time

Learning new skills takes time and you may have to respond to your child consistently like this a number of times.

Eventually your child will learn different ways of expressing their feelings.

Where to get advice

Contact your public health nurse, GP or GP practice nurse for more advice on coping with your child's developing behaviour.

If you are finding your child's behaviour stressful

Talk to your partner or a friend if you are feeling stressed, angry or upset about your child's behaviour.

If you feel you need more support or advice, contact:

- your local family resource centre
- your public health nurse
- your GP
- your GP practice nurse
- Parentline on 1890 927 277

Sharing

Sharing is an important skill that your child will need for school. They will also need this skill to help them get along with other children.

Don't expect smaller children to share. They don't usually develop this skill until they're between the ages of three and four. Smaller children will need lots of help to learn how to share and there are things you can do to help your child.

Helping your child learn to share

Keep an eye on your child when they are playing with other children.

Talk calmly and work it out

If the children begin fighting over a toy, game or book, calmly talk to them. Try to work through the conflict with them. With an older child, support them in trying to solve the problem or conflict themselves.

Keep an eye on your child

If they are about to grab a toy from another child, squat down beside them and ask them what the problem is. Ask what happened and repeat it so you are sure you understand what has just happened from their point of view. Ask them for their ideas on a solution to the problem. Choose a practical solution together.

Remove the cause of the fight

If children continue fighting over a toy or activity, remove it for a short time. Explain that you expect them to play nicely. Tell them you will return the toy or activity when they calm down. When you return it, explain the rules again. If the fighting happens again take it away again – this time for longer.

Ways to practice sharing

- Play games with your child where they must wait to take their turn – such as playing on a swing.

- Colour pictures and share a packet of crayons. They have to wait to use a colour if you are already using it.

- Remind them to say 'please' if they want something. Praise them for asking nicely and waiting their turn.

- For older children, play board games like snakes and ladders. Your child learns that they may not always win, but they can enjoy taking part in a group-based game. They also see other children or adults win or lose without getting upset.

Sibling rivalry

It is normal for your older child or children to feel jealous at the arrival of a new brother or sister.

Many young children:

- go back to 'baby' behaviour, such as a child who is fully toilet trained wetting themselves again

- have tantrums again

What to do

The time and love you give to your older child or children and the way you deal with their behaviour is important. It is also crucial that they learn how to deal with other emotions as they grow.

Here are some tips to help your older child cope:

- Be patient and understanding with them.
- Try to keep the family routine as normal as possible for your older child.
- Encourage your older child to become involved, especially during times of play and reading.
- Do not force your older child to be too involved. They may not want to help.
- Your child will still need special one-on-one time with you to help them feel loved and secure. Try and make time for this each day, even if it's only for 10 or 15 minutes.

Anxiety

It is normal for children to feel anxious about different things as they grow. Fears and worries are a normal part of life. Common fears in childhood include animals, insects, storms, water and the dark. These fears usually go away gradually on their own.

From about seven months to the age of three, children can be clingy, and can cry when separated from you. This is called separation anxiety.

Separation anxiety

Separation anxiety is a normal part of your child's development. Nearly all children experience separation anxiety at some stage. For some it may last longer than others.

Separation anxiety is a sign that your child knows how important you are to them. It shows that they have a strong attachment to you. But it can be very upsetting for parents.

You can help your child to understand and cope with their feelings. With your help, your child will learn that they will be ok and that you will return. Leaving your child with another caregiver is not going to damage them. It actually teaches them how to cope without you. This helps them to become more independent.

How to manage separation anxiety

Remember this will pass. Separation anxiety is completely normal. As your child gets older, they learn that you continue to exist even when you are out of sight.

Until that happens, don't let their separation anxiety stop them from having new experiences or spending time with friends. Don't let it stop you doing the things you need to do, like going to work or going shopping.

Try to leave your child with familiar people

If you are arranging new childcare, arrange a few visits to give your child the chance to get to know the new minder or minders while with you. Gradually build up the time your child spends with them.

Let your child know what you will do together later

This gives them something to look forward to. For example: "When Mammy comes back we are going to visit Nanny's house."

Leave something comforting with your child

Sometimes a scarf that smells like you, or a favourite toy can reassure your child while you are away.

Make saying goodbye a positive time

Smile and say goodbye in a confident happy way. Don't let your child see that you are sad or worried. Never sneak away without saying goodbye. Try to remember that through your saying goodbye and returning, your child is learning that when you leave, you will return.

Know when to get help

If your child remains upset for a long time after you leave, if they are very distressed, or if it is going on for a few weeks, speak to your GP or public health nurse.

Planning a short break away from your child

If you are planning a short break away from your child, prepare well in advance.

Ways to help you to prepare your child:

- Let your child know you are going away two or three days before you go. Then they have time to ask questions and prepare themselves.
- Talk about it as a positive experience for your child: "Isn't it great you are going for a sleep-over with Granny?"
- Make sure a responsible adult looks after your child while you are gone.
- Discuss your child's routine with the person who will care for them. Include information on your child's favourite food, their favourite bedtime story and their toilet training routine.
- If possible, don't separate your children between different homes when you go away. They may already feel upset about being away from you.
- Reassure your child that you will be coming back soon and say goodbye to them rather than slipping out so that they understand that you are gone.
- Keep in touch with your child by phone or video calls.

Development of your child's sexuality

When you hear the word "sexuality", you may think about sexual activity and contact. However, it is about much more than this. It is about how we develop physically and emotionally, how we express ourselves and how we form relationships with others.

The messages that children get from birth about the human body and intimacy will influence their future development so it's important that you consider what you'd like those messages to be.

Age	Your child may:
From 2 to 3 years	<ul><li>still be trying to work out how parts of their body are connected to the rest of them</li><li>be trying to figure out how their body works</li></ul>
From 3 to 5 years	<ul><li>be modest about their body</li><li>like being naked</li><li>be interested in looking at their own body and at other children's bodies</li><li>be interested in their parents' bodies and how they differ from their own</li><li>ask you about the different parts of your own body and want to touch them</li><li>want to know where babies come from</li><li>like touching their own private parts when they are upset or tense or as a comfort when they are going to sleep</li></ul>

Birth to 3 years

Your young child learns their first lessons from being cuddled by you. So it's important to show love to them with hugs and kisses.

They also learn about things through touch, including touching their own bodies. By accepting these explorations, you will show them that their body is normal. If you correct them for touching themselves, they will start to feel something is wrong with that part of their body.

Your young child thinks that whatever happens in their family must be the right way of doing things. So don't be afraid to kiss and hug your partner in front of your child if you want to.

3 to 5 years

By this age your child is aware and curious about the differences between the sexes. They also have a natural curiosity about their own and other people's bodies.

They may show their curiosity as part of their overall playtime. For example, they may play doctors and nurses to explore their own and other young children's bodies in a safe way.

The questions they often ask at this age include: "Where do babies come from?" and "Can daddy have babies too?" You can reply by asking them a question such as "Where do you think babies come from?" This way you find out what they already know. A short and truthful answer is all you need.

Talk about babies and bodies in a language and at a level that they can understand – for example how a mother's body changes when she is expecting a baby; how her breasts make milk to feed the new baby.

You can use picture books about the body to help you discuss the subject. Reading your child stories often helps them talk about different feelings and relationships.

Use everyday situations to start a conversation about sex and relationships. Topics on TV programmes are also a good opportunity to start the chat. Or talk when you're tidying up around the home so your child feels that sex and development are a normal part of family life.

How to support your child as they learn about their body

Think before you say anything so you don't make your child feel ashamed. For example, if you say "no" or "that's dirty" in a cross way when you see your young child touch their genitals, they will think that touching and exploring their own body is bad.

Name all the body parts including the bum, penis, scrotum and vulva when you bathe your child. Tell them that any touching they may do needs to be done in private.

Try to work out if anything might be worrying your child. You must also be alert to times when they may be exposed to harm.

Encourage them to tell you if they feel uncomfortable or unsafe in any situation or with any person. Always believe your child and seek help if you are concerned.

Contact your GP for more information about, and support with, the development of your child's sexuality.

> See sexualwellbeing.ie for advice and resources for parents of young children.

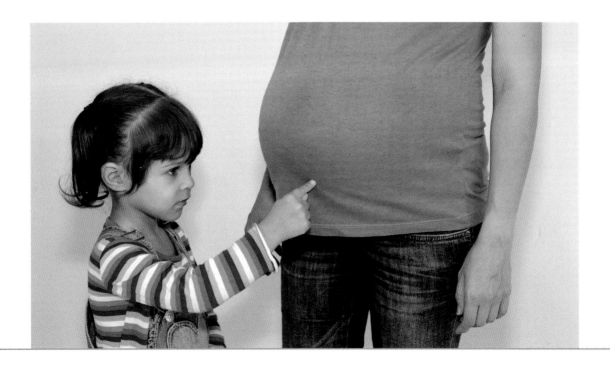

Playing, being active and learning

Playing and being active can help your child to have a healthy body, develop self-confidence and improve their ability to learn and pay attention.

Helping your child to stay active

Staying fit and healthy is important for your child's normal growth and development. It also helps you and your family keep well. Being active and having a healthy balanced diet with enough sleep are all part of staying fit and healthy.

Physical activity

Children under five should have at least three hours of physical activity spread throughout the day, building up to at least one hour of energetic play by five years of age.

The activity doesn't need to be all at once. It can be built up over the course of the day. All activity counts – walking, running, dancing, hopping, skipping or cycling. Reducing the amount of time your child is sitting or not moving also matters.

> **What you can do**
> - Create safe places to play.
> - Play music and learn action songs together.
> - Dress for the weather and explore the outdoors.
> - Make time for play with other children.
> - Whenever possible, get where you're going by walking or cycling – even doing part of the journey on foot or by bike will make a difference.
> - Try to have screen-free zones in the home or screen-free times during the day.

Learning through play

Play is important for children because it is how they learn and develop. Play is a child's 'work'. Playing with your child can help you build a close and satisfying relationship with them.

As a busy parent, you may need to plan playtime with your child so as not to miss out on it. The play session doesn't have to be long to be useful.

It is very common these days for children to be around a lot of electronic devices. Take the time to encourage your child to play with traditional, slower-paced toys and games so as to build their concentration levels. Model this by playing board games or going on nature walks and pointing things out.

Your child learns the importance of building play with you into their daily routine and they look forward to this.

With children up to six years old, a short session of 15 minutes can make a difference to their lives. Set aside time to play after mealtimes and have wind down time before bedtime such as reading or doing jigsaws together. Even if your child has misbehaved during the day, have uninterrupted playtime with them.

How play helps your child to grow and develop

Development	What your child learns to do
Physical	**2 to 5 years** Play releases your child's need for physical activity and ensures that they get enough to help their health and development.
Intellectual	**2 to 3 years** Your child uses their imagination. For example, they might drink tea out of a pretend cup.  **3 to 5 years** Your child's thinking skills develop. They start to count toys with the numbers 1, 2 and 3. They know the differences in sizes like big and small.

Development	What your child learns to do
Emotional and behavioural	**2 to 3 years** Your child learns to communicate. They start to show concern towards other children around the same age as them, by feeling concern for them or becoming distressed by the other's distress. **3 to 5 years** Your child is beginning to learn how to deal with emotions. They let themselves be comforted by less familiar adults such as their friend's mother or their schoolteacher. Your child is more likely to fear some things at this stage, such as dogs or darkness. Empathy continues to develop gradually. Around ages 4 to 5 your child may start to think about what another person is experiencing or to take the perspective of others.
Social	**2 to 3 years** Playing encourages their sense of independence. They learn that they enjoy making friends. Playing with toys prepares them for tasks such as caring for others. **3 to 5 years** Play encourages your child to develop a separate identity. It teaches them how to get along with other children. Play encourages language development. For example, they begin to say they want something instead of using behaviours such as crying. Play with their friends becomes important. They play games such as shopkeeper or doctors and nurses with their toys. They also play games together – for example running after one another.

Developing through play

What you can do	How your child responds and what they learn
• Get down to your child's level and ask them what they want to do.	• Your child develops confidence, as they are allowed to take charge and make decisions.
• Do jigsaws and play matching games with them.	• This encourages your child to solve problems. They can find out for themselves where the jigsaw fits or what things match each other. You can help them if they need it.
• Have your child's friends around to play.	• Your child enjoys mixing and playing with other small children.
• Teach your child actions that go with songs or rhymes such as 'Head, shoulders, knees and toes' or 'Ring a ring a rosie'.	• As well as stretching and using up energy, singing and moving about teaches your child to remember words and do the matching action at the right time, such as touching their toes.
• Play chase or hide-and-seek with your child.	• Your child loves you chasing them or finding them when they hide and squeals in delight.
• Play ball games or skipping and hopping games with your child. Make obstacle courses that they have to crawl under.	• You and your child will benefit from the physical activity and you encourage them to stretch and move about.
• Go for a walk in a park or field with your child if you can. Bring the buggy (pushchair) or scooter for the journey home, as your child will become tired after a while.	• This does not cost any money and it gives your child a range of learning opportunities. For example, your child learns about nature and how things grow and live.
• Play with your child using play dough or sand and water.	• Your child will enjoy stretching or moulding the dough or the feel of wet sand and learn that it is good to get dirty.
• Encourage your child to play pretend games where they use role play.	• They enjoy pretending and using their imagination. Their communication and language skills develop as they explain what they are doing and what they 'see' around them.

What you can do	How your child responds and learns
• Pretend you and your child are animals by flapping your arms up and down like a bird flying, or hopping like a kangaroo or frog.	• Your child learns to use their imagination and gets exercise as they move about.
• Visit your local library to get a wide range of books and audio books for free.	• Audio books are useful as they will develop your child's listening skills and encourage their imagination.
• Tell your child stories about your own childhood and things you did.	• Your child will be delighted to learn more about their parents when they were small and cute.
• Allow your child to help you with cooking. They can help you roll out pastry for baking or make pancakes.	• Your child learns about different foods and how to make them. They also enjoy being praised for their tasty work.
• Let your child help you around the home by giving them a duster to shine furniture.	• They enjoy helping you out, even if your furniture may not end up very clean looking. It's the joy in taking part that is the reward and not the end result.
• Let your child know playtime will end.	• They like the chance of winding up the game instead of stopping suddenly.
• Encourage your child to tidy up after playtime. Have a place to store things.	• They feel pleased when they are capable of tidying up and you praise them.
• Discuss with your child what you did together and how much fun it was.	• This develops their speaking, listening and thinking skills.

Playing with toys and household items

Playing with a mixture of toys and everyday household items encourages your child's development. Try not to differentiate between boys' and girls' toys. Instead, offer whatever playthings you think they will enjoy.

Toys and household things you can use for play

Sand and water

- Sand, plastic jugs and cups, sieves, and a large basin of water for messy play.
- Buckets and plastic spades to dig holes in the sand, toy cars and diggers.
- Sponges to squeeze, bubbles to blow and plastic toys to wash while your child is having a bath.

Fancy dress

- Dress-up clothes such as old hats and scarves, shirts or colourful dresses, wellington boots, slippers and gloves, a doctor's white coat and bag, or super hero cape.

Toys

- A tricycle or a small bicycle with side stabilisers, or a scooter to move about on.
- Big and small balls to bounce, kick and roll on the floor.
- A little kitchen area with empty food packets, plastic cups, a pretend cooker, a rolling pin and a wooden spoon.
- A workbench with a plastic hammer, toy tool set and hard hat for your child to wear while they fix things.

Books

- Colourful storybooks with stories about people from different cultures.
- Books about things that happen around them such as the arrival of a new baby, going into hospital or starting school.
- Visit your local library together.

Art and crafts

- Non-toxic paint and colourful crayons to help create shapes and figures.
- Stencil patterns so your child can draw and discover different shapes and how to create them.

- Finger paints so they can use their fingers to feel the textures of the paint on the page.
- Let them stick up the picture they drew. This shows your child that you are proud of the work they have done.

Outdoors
- A window box or a small area in the garden where your child can dig the soil and grow flowers from bulbs or seeds.

Toy safety
Check that all toys and items are safe and the right size for your child to play with.

Check for the CE mark (safety symbol).

Throw out broken toys. They can be dangerous.

On long trips and journeys
Long trips can make your child bored and likely to misbehave. Prepare by planning for story-telling, songs, I-spy games and having toys and snacks available.

Plan to take small breaks in safe areas where your child can stretch their legs and run around.

Always make sure your child is securely strapped into a car seat that is right for their height and weight. Strap them in even for short journeys.

Screen time

Screen time is the time your child spends in front of a screen including watching programmes and videos and interacting with applications (apps) on TV, tablets or phones.

Screens and devices are hard to avoid. More research is needed to fully understand whether screen time and interacting with technology can be good for a child's development. However, there is evidence available on how screen time can have a negative impact on your child's development if they often spend a lot of time in front of a screen.

Too much screen time means they could be more likely to:
- sleep less and have sleep issues
- be overweight or obese
- have poorer language skills
- have poorer cognitive skills – for example, issues with their attention

Your child might experience these issues because the more time they spend in front of a screen, the less time they spend on activities which are key to their development. These include playing, moving around, being active and interacting with those around them.

Evidence also suggests that having a TV on in the background can have a negative impact on your child's development.

How to make the most out of screen time

- Sit with your child when they are playing on an app or watching a programme – talk to them about what they are doing and what they see and how it relates to the world around them.
- Choose high-quality programmes or apps that are appropriate for your child's age. Visit commonsensemedia.org – this site helps parents make smart media choices for children from the age of 24 months and up.
- Try to choose apps that can involve you and that have automatic stops or pauses – this will make it easier to set limits on the time your child spends on the app.
- Test apps before your child uses them so you know what they involve.

Many apps are advertised as educational but there is very little evidence to back up these claims – check commonsensemedia.org and do your own research.

How to avoid problems associated with screen time

Set limits on your child's screen time

Between the ages of two and five, it is recommended that they spend no more than one hour a day in front of a screen.

Be with them

Make sure your child is in the same room as you when they are on a device so that you can monitor what they are watching or playing.

Have screen-free times and zones

Make meal-times screen-free zones. Keep the hour before bedtime screen-free. Avoid having screens, including TVs, in your child's bedroom.

Turn off screens nobody is using

Turn off screens in the background when they are not in use as they can still distract children and get in the way of their playing and learning.

Keep an eye on the rest of the family's screen use

Be aware of how much time you and the rest of your family spend on screen time. Your child will notice what you and other family members do and will try to copy it.

Avoid relying on a screen to calm your child down

Learning to calm themselves is an important part of their development. If you are having trouble calming your child, please see tips on pages 88 to 92.

Avoid using screens to distract your child when you are busy

Instead, set them up safely with an appropriate toy or activity or involve them in what you are doing. For example, get them to help when you are making a meal.

Staying safe online

Always supervise your child when they're online. As you and your child interact with the wider online community, teach them about respecting others online. It is also important to teach your child about staying safe online. From an early age teach them not to interact with strangers online.

Removing geotags is something that some parents like to do. A geotag has geographical information about where a photo was taken or where a social media post was uploaded. Having a geotag on a photo could allow a stranger to find your home, your favourite park or your child's playgroup. If you are on holidays, a photo with a geotag that you share on social media could potentially alert burglars to the fact that your home is empty.

Keeping your child safe

As your child grows, they become more adventurous. While they are busy exploring the world, they rely on you to make sure they are safe.

Teaching safety without scaring your child

If you tell your child not to talk to strangers, you might confuse or frighten them. They don't know who you really mean because you may also be encouraging your child to be polite to new people they meet when they are out with you.

For example, a new parent at the preschool or a shopkeeper are all strangers when we first meet them, but you want your child to be polite and friendly to them.

Instead, teach your child that they must never go off on their own, or off with another person, until they tell you about it. If someone else is minding them, your child needs to know that they should tell their minder what is happening. Here are two examples.

Example 1:

Your child is playing on the slide in the park. They want to move to a slide that is further away. Your child should come back and check with you before they move. Then you know where they are at all times.

Example 2:

Your child is playing with their good friend from next door. Their friend's parent wants to bring them both to the local shop for some snacks. They should come back and check with you. You can then decide if it is ok for them to go or not.

This rule does not stop your child from becoming more independent as they grow.

Instead, it helps to keep them safe. Your child must learn not to trust anybody who tries to lure them into a car or anybody who wants to walk away with them.

Unintentional injuries

Most unintentional injuries (accidents) to children under five years of age happen in their own home. The good news is that, with a little planning, you can prevent most of these injuries.

Never underestimate your child's ability and speed

Your child will learn very quickly how to climb and get to things that may have been out of reach before.

When people come and go from your home, be aware of where your child is at all times. Hold their hand securely when people are driving into or out of the driveway. Keep the front and back door closed at all times.

Constant supervision

The key message underpinning child safety is constant adult supervision. In other words, watch your child at all times as children do not understand danger.

First aid

Keep a well-stocked first aid kit at home. Store it out of sight and reach of your children. Do not store medicines in the first aid kit. Store them separately in a locked high cupboard.

Wall chart

Your public health nurse gave you a HSE child safety wall chart. It includes some basic first aid steps for common injuries. Familiarise yourself with these steps but get medical attention if in any doubt.

Be prepared

The Irish Red Cross has an app with easy-to-follow tips for more than 20 common first aid scenarios. It also gives advice about how to prepare for emergency situations, including floods, fires and water safety. See the app store or redcross.ie

If you get a chance, do a first aid course. For information you can contact the Order of Malta, the Irish Red Cross or St John's Ambulance. Your public health nurse may also know of first aid courses being run in your area.

Emergency services

In an emergency

Phone 999 or 112 to contact:

- the ambulance service
- fire service
- Garda Síochana
- the Irish Coast Guard

Know your Eircode

It is a good idea to make a list of easy-to-follow directions to your home and put them where you and others can see them.

Your Eircode can help emergency services to find your home faster. Make a note of your Eircode and put it somewhere obvious in case you or someone else in your home needs to give it to 999 or 112 in an emergency. See eircode.ie

Childproofing your home inside and outside

Childproofing your home is one of the most valuable actions you can take to help keep your child safe. It helps you spot potential dangers so that you can take action to fix them.

> The best way to childproof your home is to:
>
> - get down on your knees to your child's height
> - look at every area of your home (inside and outside) through their eyes
> - ask yourself: "Is there anything here that could be a danger to my child?"
> - check for dangers that they can climb to
> - remove the dangers once you have identified them

Your public health nurse gave you a HSE child safety checklist. You should use this to guide you. Aim to have every box ticked and a plan to fix anything you have not ticked.

Childproof regularly

Childproofing is not a once-off activity. You need to repeat it regularly as your child learns new skills.

Put safety measures in place before your child reaches their next developmental stage.

Child safety equipment

Safety equipment does not replace the need for adult supervision. However, it can make protecting your child easier.

Equipment you should have

At windows
- Secure all windows with restrictors that do not need tools for opening (so you can escape in case of fire).

Open fires, stoves and heaters (see page 116)
- Sparkguards.
- Fireguards.

Stairs
- Stair gates at top and bottom of stairs – remove when your child is able to climb over them.

On TVs and furniture
- Brackets or straps to secure TVs and stands, chests of drawers, bookcases and other free-standing furniture to the wall or floor.
- Furniture pads to cover sharp corners on furniture.

On cupboards
- Cupboard locks.
- Drawer locks.

In the kitchen
- Fridge and freezer locks.
- Fire blanket.
- Fire extinguisher.

In the bathroom
- Non-slip bath mat.
- Toilet locks.

Alarms
- Smoke alarms.
- Carbon monoxide alarms.

On doors
- Safety door stoppers (but never on fire doors).

First aid and emergency information
- Well-stocked first aid kit.
- Basic first aid instructions.
- Emergency contact numbers.
- HSE child safety wall chart.

Other items
- Room thermometer.
- Bath thermometer.
- 5-way safety harness on seating devices.

When buying and using equipment
Make sure:

- it meets current safety standards
- it is in perfect condition
- you assemble, install and use it correctly – follow the manufacturer's instructions

Soften sharp corners and hard edges

Use furniture pads to cover any sharp corners in the home. Soften hard edges like window sills with cushion corners. Position hard items like wooden holdbacks for curtains so that your child can't run into them.

Sharing child safety information

Share safety information with everyone who takes care of your child – grandparents, aunts, uncles, friends, childminders and baby sitters. This will make sure you are all on the same page when it comes to your child's safety.

Lead by example

Always act safely. From the earliest age, children learn from what we do, not just what we say. So model safe behaviour at all times around them.

Talk to your child about safety

Speak to your child regularly about safety. If you sow the seeds of safety at an early age it will prepare your child so they can understand how important it is to put safety first as they grow older.

Set clear and simple safety rules that children can understand. For example:

- "Inside we walk."
- "Our toys stay on the ground when we climb."
- "We put away our toys when we've finished playing."
- "We climb up the ladder and come down the slide."
- "We always wear our helmet when on our bike or scooter."

Remember that rules are not a replacement for supervision. They are simply a way of teaching children what it is safe to do.

Remind your child of the safety information you have shared with them when they are near, in or at that particular area of safety. For example, when crossing the road with your child, remind them about the safe cross code.

Congratulate them as they learn new safety tips and, in particular, when they put them into practice.

Never expect your child to take responsibility for their safety. Children do not understand danger. Parents and carers are responsible for making their child's world as safe as possible.

Preventing common childhood injuries

Falls

Did you know?

About 50% of all unintentional injuries in children under 5 are caused by falls. It is the most common cause of injury in children who have to go to hospital.

Windows and balconies

Secure all windows with window restrictors. Get the type that don't need you to use tools to open them. That way, you can escape quickly in a fire. Avoid placing beds, cots, toy boxes or other furniture near any window where a child could climb up and fall out.

Secure balcony doors and get rid of or block any gaps in balcony railings that a child could fit through or use as a foothold to climb. Do not place anything children could climb on near balcony railings like outdoor furniture, plant pots or boxes.

TVs and furniture

Make sure furniture is safely positioned to prevent falls from climbing. Keep bedroom furniture to a minimum to limit climbing opportunities.

TVs, bookcases, chests of drawers, coat stands and other free-standing equipment and furniture can cause serious or fatal injury if they or their contents fall on your child. Always secure these items to the wall or floor using brackets or straps.

Avoid placing TVs on top of cabinets and chests of drawers as your child may climb into one of the drawers to reach the screen. Make sure items such as kitchen units, dressers, mirrors, fireplaces and mantelpieces are correctly secured to the wall.

Bunk beds

Do not allow children to play on bunk beds. Position bunk beds away from windows, ceiling lights, fans and furniture. Carpeting the floor can decrease the risk of head injury from a bunk bed fall.

Bunk bed dangers include:

- Falls from the top bunk, from the ladder or from windows near the bed.
- Suffocation if a child slips between the guard rail and mattress.
- Heads or limbs getting caught or trapped between parts of the bed or in gaps and crevices.
- Strangulation or accidental hanging when a child's head or neck is caught up in clothing, gaps or other objects on or near the bed. These objects include a cord or rope tied to the bed or located near the bed.

Children should be at least 6 years old before they are allowed on the top bunk bed.

Floors

Running in socks on a shiny or wooden floor can lead to a nasty fall – encourage your child to wear well-fitting slippers or go barefoot inside the home.

Stair gates

Install stair gates correctly and keep them closed. Use stair gates at both the top and bottom of stairs and other areas that pose a trip hazard — like steps at doorways or changes in floor level. Remove stair gates once your child is able to climb over them.

Show your child how to slowly and safely climb the stairs. Keep steps and staircases clear.

Other hazards

Reduce hazards by ensuring that walls are finished correctly, that gates are in good working order and there is no equipment or items lying around that your child could climb onto.

Store ladders away safely – out of sight and reach of children. Be very aware of the risks to your child when carrying out work to your home or during renovations.

Fire safety

Children are fascinated by fire, matches and candles and do not understand danger.

Fire alarms

Have working smoke alarms in the hall and landing and aim to have one in every room.

Test regularly (once a week is advised) and replace wasted batteries immediately. Make a fire escape plan and practice it often.

Fireguards

Use a fireguard and a sparkguard on open fires. Stoves and heaters should be protected by a fireguard. Fireguards should be secured to a wall. Never place anything on a fireguard.

Candles

Avoid using candles while your child is indoors. When you do use them, position candles in a safe place away from draughts, fabrics or anything else that could catch fire. Avoid moving a lit candle.

Matches and lighters

Keep matches and lighters out of your child's reach and sight.

Sockets

Never overload sockets. Switch off and unplug electrical equipment when not in use.

Chip pans

Traditional cooker top chip pans are a fire risk. Consider a different method of cooking.

Burns and scalds

Burns and scalds can lead to serious injuries which often need prolonged treatment and skin grafts. Keep kettles, hot drinks and hot liquids out of reach of children.

Cookers

Use a cooker guard for protection. Always cook on back rings first, with saucepan handles turned in. Make sure your child stays away from the cooker when it's in use and teach them why this is important.

Hot drinks and foods

Keep hot drinks out of your child's reach. It only takes a small amount of liquid to cover a child's face and torso, causing devastating injuries.

Avoid using tablecloths as children can pull hot drinks down with them.

Use a short flex on your kettle and other electrical equipment.

Never hold your child while you're making or drinking hot drinks or while cooking.

Electrical items

Keep all electrical equipment and flexes out of your child's reach.

Hot water

Always run cold water first and then add the warm water. If your bath has a single tap with a hot and cold feed, make sure you run the cold water again to cool the taps so they won't burn your child.

Test the water with elbow or bath thermometer before putting your child into the bath. It should be between 37°C to 38°C. Never leave your child alone in the bath.

Choking

Children under three are at the highest risk of choking due to small size of their respiratory tract. Keep small and unsuitable items they might choke on out of their reach.

Preparing food

Always cut up food to a size that your child can chew and eat safely.

If you need to make chewing easier, change the texture of the food – grate, cook, finely chop or mash it.

Remove the parts of food that could choke your child – peel off the skin or remove any strong fibres.

Small fruit and vegetables

Grapes, cherry tomatoes and other similar-sized food can choke your child. Cut them into quarters lengthways or smaller.

Hard fruit and vegetables

These include carrots, celery and apples. If you need to make chewing easier, change the texture of the food – grate, cook, finely chop or mash it.

Food with skins or leaves

Food skins are difficult to chew and can completely seal children's airways. They include:

- sausages, hot dogs and frankfurters
- apples and pears
- tomatoes
- lettuce and other raw salad leaves
- spinach and cabbage

Remove or peel skins and cut lengthways into small pieces no bigger than your child's small fingernail. Add to mashed food. Finely chop salad leaves. Cook spinach and cabbage until soft and chop finely.

Fruit with stones

Remove the stone from fruits like plums, peaches and nectarines. Peel and cut as above.

Thick pastes and spreads

Thick pastes like peanut butters and chocolate spreads can stick to your child's throat and windpipe, making breathing difficult. Spread pastes thinly and evenly.

Never give your child the following foods as they could choke:

- whole nuts
- marshmallows
- chewing gum
- boiled sweets
- popcorn

Eating

Always supervise your child when they are eating. Do not let them put too much food into their mouth at any one time. Always remove your child's bib after they have eaten. Bibs can be a strangulation risk during sleep or play.

Food on the go

Children should sit still while eating. Your child is more likely to choke if they are walking or running around. Never allow children to run with sharp objects, food or lollipops.

Bed-time eating

Never allow your child to eat or drink in bed as it increases the risk that they will choke.

Batteries

Keep all remote controls and spare or used batteries in a secure place. Make sure all battery compartments on toys and other items are secure and can't be opened by little hands.

Button batteries

Your child may not choke after swallowing a button battery but if undetected it could seriously burn their insides. Go to hospital immediately if you think your child has swallowed one or put one in their ear or nose.

Balloons

Only adults should inflate balloons – children as old as 12 have choked after the balloon they were inflating got stuck in their throat. Children can also choke on uninflated balloons and pieces of broken balloons.

Toys

Use the right toy for your child's age and stage of development and look for the CE mark. Throw away broken toys.

Common choking hazards

When something gets stuck

Your child could get an item stuck in their eyes, ears or nose. Signs may include redness, irritation, pain, bleeding, discharge or a bad smell.

Never try to remove objects that are stuck in your child's ears, eyes or nose as this could cause them a serious injury. Always seek medical advice.

An object stuck in your child's nose can cause breathing difficulties or choking if they breathe it in. Go to your nearest hospital emergency department if your child starts having difficulty breathing.

Strangulation

Blind cords, curtain cords and clothing (like ribbons and belts) can put your child at serious risk of strangulation.

Blinds and curtain cords

Do not fit blinds or curtains with cords attached. Replace cords with curtain or blind wands. It will help to prevent an eye injury to your child if you keep wands out of their reach.

If it's not possible to remove cords, cord tie down or tension devices can pull the cord tight and secure it to the wall or floor. This reduces the chance that your child might be strangled by the continuous loop cords often found on vertical blinds.

Clothing and jewellery

Children are at risk of strangulation from anything placed around their neck or that catches around their neck. Never place any of the following on your child:

- jewellery (including teething jewellery)
- hair bands
- strings
- cords
- belts
- ribbons
- clips
- ties
- clothes and hats with strings or cords attached

Wires and flexes

Keep electrical flexes and phone chargers out of reach.

Strings, cords and rope

Never allow your child to play with string, cords or ropes.

Railings, banisters and other gaps

Beware of the risk of getting trapped or strangled posed by railings, banisters and any fittings, fixtures or furniture with gaps.

Bunk beds

Strangulation or accidental hanging is a risk whenever a child's head or neck is caught in clothing, gaps in furniture or other objects on or near a bunk bed – for example on a cord or rope. Heads or limbs can get caught or trapped between parts of the bed or in gaps and crevices.

Suffocation

Plastic materials

Store plastic nappy sacks and bags, plastic bags, dry-cleaning and other plastic packaging out of reach. Plastic material can cling to your child's face and suffocate them.

Water safety

Drowning

Drowning is a leading cause of death in children. Watch your child at all times as children can stray very quickly and fall into water. Always make sure your child is within your sight and arm's reach.

> Never leave your child alone near, with or in water – not even for a second. Drowning can happen in silence (without any splashing or screaming), in an instant and in a very small amount of water.

Children who survive near-drowning frequently have long-term health effects from brain injury.

Water containers

Use protective covers and fence off water collecting containers. Watch your child at all times as they can wander very quickly. Fence off man-made ponds, garden streams and open water areas.

Paddling pools

Empty paddling pools immediately after use and store them in a locked shed.

Bath-time

Never leave your child alone at bath time, even for a second. If you need to leave, bring your child with you. Always empty the bath as soon as you remove your child.

Swimming aids

Make sure arm bands and other buoyancy aids have an approved safety standard mark (IS EN 13138 and the CE mark), fit properly and are appropriate for your child's age and developmental stage. Even if they are wearing an armband, your child will need constant adult supervision.

Pools

If you are near a swimming pool, be very careful. Make sure there is a locked gate or door separating your child from the pool. Even if the pool has a lifeguard, your child will still need parental supervision.

Introduce your child to swimming as early as possible.

Poisons

Medicine and supplements

Keep all medicines and vitamin supplements in original containers and lock them in an overhead medicine cabinet or high cupboard.

Follow instructions on medicine labels carefully. Return old and unused medicines to your chemist.

Store herbal, iron and vitamin tablets or supplements, including 'gummy bear' type supplements given to older children, out of reach. Iron supplements are very dangerous for young children if taken in a high dose. Don't use the word 'sweets' when talking about medicines or vitamins.

Child-resistant caps on medicines are not childproof. Keep medicine out of reach at all times.

Detergents and cleaning products

Store chemicals and household cleaning and laundry products (including laundry and dishwater tablets, capsules and pods) in high cupboards. Use cupboard safety locks.

Garden and DIY products

Keep garden and DIY products in original containers and out of reach in a locked shed. Dispose of old and unused chemicals and products safely.

Never use soft drink bottles for storage. Always keep household products in their original child-resistant containers – but be aware that child-resistant containers are not childproof.

Handbag items

Place all handbags out of your child's reach as they may contain tablets, chewing gum, hand gel, cosmetics or perfume.

E-cigarettes

Do not leave electronic cigarettes or their refills in reach or sight of children. These products contain nicotine, which is highly toxic when swallowed or inhaled by children.

Syringes and needles

Keep syringes and needles locked away and dispose of them safely after use.

Carbon monoxide

Use carbon monoxide alarms (EN 50291 standard) in every room with a fuel-burning appliance.

Poisonous plants

Remove any poisonous plants indoors and from your garden. Get advice from your garden centre when buying plants to make sure they are not a danger to your child.

Public Poisons Line

If you think that your child has taken poison, stay calm but act quickly. Contact the Public Poisons Information Helpline by ringing (01) 809 2166. Save this number to your phone.

Your call will be answered by a specialist who will tell you if your child needs medical attention. The helpline is open every day from 8am to 10pm. See poisons.ie

Outside of these hours, contact your GP or hospital. In an emergency, call 999 or 112.

Sun

If your child's skin is exposed to too much sun, this may increase their risk of skin cancer later in life. Too much sun can also cause cataracts in adulthood and cancer in the eye. UV rays can pass through light clouds.

Cover up

Dress your child in loose-fitting, long-sleeved, light protective clothing made from close-woven fabric that doesn't let sunlight through. Use a wide-brimmed sunhat that protects the face, neck and ears.

Find shade

Keep your child out of direct sunlight as much as possible (especially between 11am to 3pm). Use a sunshade on your buggy.

Use sunscreen

- Choose a UVA and UVB sunscreen made for children with at least SPF 30.
- Patch test it on their skin first. Try sunscreen for sensitive skin if irritation occurs.
- For best protection, apply sunscreen at least 20 minutes before going out in the sun. Cover all exposed areas, including the face, ears, nose, lips and tops of the feet.
- Reapply sun screen (including 'waterproof' and 'water-resistant' products) at least every two hours, especially after your child swims or plays outdoors.

Sunglasses

Protect your child's eyes with sunglasses as close to 100% UV protection as possible. Wraparound style offers the best protection.

Keep hydrated

Make sure your child drinks enough fluid. Children cannot adjust to changes in temperature as well as adults. They sweat less, reducing their ability to cool down.

Facts about tanning

A tan does not protect your skin from sunburn. There is no such thing as a healthy tan. Any tan can increase your risk of developing skin cancer. Even when a tan fades, the skin damage caused by tanning never goes.

Getting sunburnt in childhood or adolescence can increase the risk of melanoma – the most serious form of skin cancer – in later life.

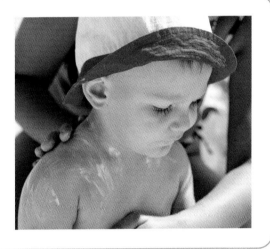

Car seats

By law all children under 150cms and 36kgs must use the right car seat for their height and weight. Child car seats must conform to EU standards. Never use a second-hand car seat unless you are sure of its safety history.

In Ireland, four out of five car seats for children are not properly fitted, which can lead to serious injury or even death in a crash. Get expert help when fitting your car seat. The Road Safety Authority offers a free 'check it fits' service – see rsa.ie

Make sure your child is secured in a properly fitted car seat for every journey, no matter how short.

Rearward facing

Keep your child in a rearward-facing seat for as long as possible. This will give greater protection to their head, neck and spine. Rearward-facing baby seats are suitable for children weighing less than 13kg. Extended rearward-facing seats are suitable for children weighing 9 to 25kg. See rsa.ie for more information about car seats.

Do not use the front seat if possible

It is safer for children to travel in the back seat in their appropriate child car seat. Never place your child in a <u>rearward facing car seat</u> in the front passenger seat where there is an active frontal air bag. It is very dangerous and also illegal.

The RSA advises: "Think carefully about driving with a child in the front seat – <u>even in the forward position</u>. You must make sure that the passenger seat is rolled back as far away from the dashboard as possible".

Clothing and the harness

Your child's clothing can affect how the harness on their car seat fits. Use blankets instead of bulky jackets in cooler weather. This makes sure the harness is making contact with your child's body.

The harness should be tight enough so only two of your fingers can fit between the top of your child's shoulders and the harness straps. Your fingers should be unable to rotate (turn) in that position. Check this before every journey.

Parked car

Never leave your child alone in a parked car, not even for a short time. Always remove your car keys from your car and keep it locked. Keep your keys out of sight and reach of children.

Outdoors

Never allow your child access to the road or to pathways beyond your home without adult supervision. Keep outside gates closed and locked and ensure there are no gaps in the surrounding fence or wall. Remove objects near gates and walls that children could climb onto.

Driveways

Due to their small size, children are at risk from reversing vehicles. When vehicles are coming into or leaving your driveway, make sure your children are safely inside the home, or securely in an adult's arms, or their hand is being held by an adult.

External doors

Keep all external doors locked. The keys should be out of sight and reach of children but near the door in case of a fire.

Garden machinery

Keep children well away from lawnmowers, strimmers and other garden machinery.

Ladders

Store ladders away safely – out of sight and reach of children.

Play equipment

Check the equipment is:

- suitable for your child's age and developmental stage
- in good condition
- secured to the ground with no sharp edges or bits sticking out
- carrying a recognised safety symbol such as the CE mark

Locate play equipment in a safe area not too near walls, trees, tree houses or hard surfaces such as tarmac, decking or paths, or near places where children might try to jump on or off.

Trampolines

Trampolines should have safety padding and safety nets. Assemble according to manufacturer's instructions and make sure you install all the safety features it needs. Children under six should not be allowed on a trampoline. Do not have more than one person on a trampoline at a time.

Cycling and walking

Your child should wear a helmet on scooters and bicycles and reflective clothing when cycling. Their bike should have a working bell and front and back lights if they are going to use it on or near the road.

Make sure you and your child wear reflective clothing at night and when visibility is poor (for example rainy, misty, foggy conditions or at sunrise and sunset).

Always hold your child's hand when crossing the road or when walking near traffic.

Pets

Never leave your young child alone with a dog, cat or any pet. This is very important whether your child is awake or sleeping and no matter how well you know the animal.

Keep all pet food and water bowls, litter trays and pet toys out of your child's reach.

Model safe behaviour and teach your child how to:

- play safely with pets
- avoid dangerous situations
- respond to danger signs
- wash their hands carefully after all contact with pets and other animals

Bites, scratches and wounds

If your child is bitten or scratched, wash the wound immediately and use disinfectant cream or solution. Always contact your GP if you are worried about a wound or if a wound is not healing properly.

Choosing a pet

Choose a pet that suits your family's lifestyle, home and outdoor space. Snakes, turtles, tortoises and lizards are not suitable pets for households which have children under the age of 5 years.

Certain breeds of dogs, and any dog with behavioural problems, will need extra care, control and supervision. Consider carefully whether a dog like that is suitable for your family.

Child safety on the farm

Working farms have many hidden dangers and children can stray very quickly. Never allow your child to play on the farm. Children are at high risk on the farm from vehicles, machinery, drowning, falls and animals.

Teach your child that the farm is a workplace and dangerous. Be extra vigilant when other children visit the farm.

Fenced-off play area

It is not possible to supervise your child safely and work on the farm at the same time. Provide your child with a child-safe, fenced–off play area, away from the working farm.

Fencing and gates should have mesh right down to the ground. This is so that children cannot climb over or slip through gates or fences. Make sure you can see the play area from inside your home and your child is supervised.

Poisons

Keep all pesticides, cleaning fluids, chemicals, veterinary medicines and equipment in their original containers and in a securely locked store. Dispose of old and unused chemicals and farm products safely. Never use soft drinks bottles to store chemicals, medicines or cleaning fluids.

Remove any poisonous plants indoors and outdoors. Get advice when buying plants to make sure they are not a danger to your child.

If you think that your child has taken poison, stay calm but act quickly. Contact the Poisons Information Helpline by ringing (01) 809 2166. The helpline is open from 8am to 10pm every day. Outside of these hours, contact your GP or hospital. In an emergency call 999 or 112.

See poisons.ie

Animals

Keep children at a safe distance from livestock and other animals.

Drowning

Use secure protective covers on barrels, troughs and tanks. Store basins and buckets out of reach of children. Empty containers can fill quickly after rainfall.

Fence off ponds and other water areas where a child could drown.

Slurry pits

Securely cover or fence all slurry facilities.

Falls

Secure gates and doors. Heavy swinging gates or doors are very dangerous, especially in high winds. Never leave ladders, replacement gates, fencing or similar objects lying around. Children may be tempted to climb.

Discourage your child from playing with bales of any description. It is very easy for children to fall from stacked bales, resulting in serious injury. They might also suffocate if they fall between bales.

Stop children from getting access to areas where they are likely to climb – for example, hay sheds, lofts, high loads, ladders, walls and gates.

Vehicles

Due to their size children are at risk from reversing vehicles. When vehicles are in use or nearby, make sure your children are safely inside the home or an adult is holding them securely in their arms or by the hand.

Never allow your child near tractors, farm vehicles or machinery. Never leave running vehicles or equipment unattended. Switch off and remove keys from all vehicles and equipment after use. Never allow your child to travel in tractors, farm vehicles or on quad bikes.

> ### Visitors
>
> Always make sure contractors and other visitors know if there are children around.

Lead by example

Lead by example by always acting safely yourself. Teach your child how to stay safe on the farm. But remember: young children do not understand danger and are not capable of being responsible for their own safety.

It's the law

The Safety, Health and Welfare at Work Act 2005 says all farmers must prepare and implement a Safety Statement. Farmers with three or fewer employees are allowed, instead, to follow the Code of Practice.

If you have a gun

You must store your gun safely where a child cannot get it. The Firearms (Secure Accommodation) Regulations 2009 tell you how you must do that.

Childcare

If you work outside the home, you will need to make childcare arrangements. These arrangements need to be right for you as a family and suit your day to day needs.

There are many factors that will make an impact on your childcare decisions.

These include:

- your child's age
- whether you need full or part-time care
- the hours you need services (regular, daytime, evenings or weekends)
- your budget
- services available in your area

Information and advice

Your city or county childcare committee

Your city or county childcare committee can provide a list of childcare providers in your area. See myccc.ie for contact details.

The Child and Family Agency (Tusla)

On tusla.ie you will find:

- a list of childcare services in your area
- tips on choosing a preschool

- inspection reports for preschool childcare facilities

Childminding Ireland

You will find a list of childminders in your area and advice on choosing a childminder at childminding.ie

Barnardos

Barnardos has a guide on what to look for called 'Quality Early Years Care and Education' which you can find on barnardos.ie

---

Types of childcare options

Full day care such as a crèche or nursery

These facilities care for children for more than 5 hours per day.

Sessional services

These services offer a planned programme of up to 3.5 hours a session. These include playschools, naíonraí (Irish language preschool or playgroup) and Montessori.

Childminders

Childminders care for children in the home. A childminder can care for up to 5 children under 6 years of age. This includes the childminder's own children if they have any. Parents and childminders arrange their own terms and conditions.

Affordable childcare

Affordable childcare is intended to provide childcare for families on lower incomes and also to support parents so they can return to work or education. Contact your local city or county childcare committee for more information on affordable childcare services in your area. See myccc.ie for contact details and affordablechildcare.ie for more information.

Early Childhood Care and Education Scheme (ECCE)

The Early Childhood Care and Education (ECCE) Scheme provides early childhood care and education for children of preschool age. See affordablechildcare.ie

If your child is upset when you leave them in preschool

Children aged three to four often get upset when they first go to preschool. Experienced preschool staff will be aware of this and will comfort your child. Here are four things you can do to help your child.

Help them adjust gradually

Help your child adjust gradually to the new place and people. Take them on short visits to their preschool well before their first day. Repeat this short visit and leave your child there for a short while.

Before you leave

Give yourself some time to stay with your child while they get comfortable.

Don't sneak out the door while your child is occupied. They will be more worried the next day if they think you're going to do that again. Even if your child is upset, it is better if they see you leave.

The important thing is to remind your child that you will be back when you say you will — then make sure you stick to that promise.

After you go

Sometimes it can be a good idea to call after an hour to see how your child is doing. More often than not, they will have settled down by then and be happily playing with their friends.

How you might feel

As a parent, it is very difficult to leave your child crying. You may feel torn between wanting to take them out of preschool to avoid their being upset and knowing that they will benefit from the social activity if you let them stay until they get used to it.

Most children adjust to a new setting. They will soon begin to enjoy the novelty and excitement of new friends, adults and things to do and see.

Preparing your child for primary school

Starting primary school is an exciting time. There is a lot you can do at home to prepare your child for this transition.

Most primary schools have a school induction where your child can go to school for a morning before they start in September. This is a great opportunity for your child to see their new school, meet their new teacher and future classmates.

You may feel emotional on the first day of school and this is all normal. It is important that your child is looking forward to starting school and that you are positive about this new life experience.

Remember that you are your child's first teacher and main carer. Read the tips in each section of this book again for suggestions on how you can help your child's development as they grow.

What to keep in mind when choosing a primary school

Speak with other parents in your area to see what schools they send their children to. Ask their opinions. Make a list of the schools you are interested in approaching.

Many schools and local areas organise enrolment events. Keep an eye on your local newspaper and the websites of the various schools in your area. Many preschools know about these events in advance and will tell you if you ask them.

When you visit the school

- Ask questions and get a tour of the school.
- Bring along your partner or a support person to share the decision-making.

Do not talk about any concerns you may have about your child starting school while they are near you. They may hear the worries and become upset.

Here are some questions to ask yourself:

- Is it a school that allows only boys or only girls, or is there a mix of both in the school?
- How many children are in each classroom?
- Do the children have to wear a uniform?
- Are different languages taught in the school?
- What policies does the school have about nutrition and exercise?
- Does the school promote a range of supervised physical activities?
- Do the teaching methods meet your child's needs?
- Does the school cater respectfully to each child's cultural background?
- Is there speech and drama to develop your child's creative side?
- Does the school offer open channels of communication? For example, will the teacher have informal chats about your child before and after school? Or do you have to wait for a planned parent teacher meeting to discuss your child's progress?
- How are children corrected when they misbehave?
- Are children praised and encouraged? This is important for their self-esteem.
- What are the academic values of the school?
- What are the spiritual and religious values of the school?

Ask to see a copy of the school's policies.

Talk to other parents about schools in your area and the parents' associations.

How to help your child prepare for school

Physical health and wellbeing

Make sure that your child has a well-balanced diet.

Spend time with your child outdoors being active.

Establish a good bedtime routine (see page 30).

Getting your child's brain and body working together helps them to learn. Encourage your child to do things like a catch a ball or hop on one foot.

Everyday tasks

There are some practical skills you can teach your child to help them be ready for school.

Teach your child to:

- put on and take off their coat and shoes
- hang up their coat
- recognise their own belongings like their lunchbox
- go to the toilet by themselves and wipe their bottom
- wash their hands
- open their lunch box and unwrap the food inside
- tidy up after themselves

Social and emotional wellbeing

Read your child a story with a problem in it and ask them about it. This will help encourage your child to think about problem solving.

Introduce your child to silent relaxation. Encourage them to close their eyes while you play soothing music in the background. Encourage them to think back about their day.

Play games with your child that encourage them to take turns and share.

Bring your young child to a parent and toddler group and then a preschool service. They will get used to mixing and sharing with others.

Make a box for dressing up that is filled with school items like a copybook, a ruler, crayons, a pencil case, an old school bag, a jumper and a lunch box. Your child will dress up in the school clothes and role-play about being in 'big school'.

Encourage and praise your child to show you believe in them.

These activities will help your child's sense of independence and confidence in school.

Learning, communication and language skills

Talk to your child about everything. For example, name everything your child sees in the garden or get them to count the number of cups on the kitchen table.

Play with your child every day. Build blocks, cut out shapes and colour pictures with thick crayons.

Play pretend games where your child uses their imagination.

Other practical things you can do

Talk about school

Talk to your child about starting school. There are some lovely books that describe a child's first day in school.

Be positive

Talk positively about your child's new school and teacher. It is not helpful to describe the teacher as someone your child should be afraid of, so try to avoid saying things like: "Miss X won't be happy if she sees you doing…"

Get to know others in the class

Get to know other children who will be starting in junior infants with your child. If possible, see if you can organise a play date with some of them.

What to get

Get a school bag that is not too heavy and is easy for your child to open and close.

Label your child's school clothes, bag, schoolbooks and lunch box so they are easy to identify if they get lost.

> ### The night before
> Get books, uniforms and lunch ready for school the night before so you and your child are not rushed in the morning.

Before school each morning

Start each day with a good healthy breakfast, such as porridge or a cereal that is low in sugar and salt. This helps your child concentrate at school.

Getting there and collection time

Allow yourself time to get to school and collect your child on time. Children get anxious if they arrive late or are left waiting.

Build a routine

Set up a routine for your child around school, homework and play time.

Your benefits and leave entitlements

There are various state benefits, schemes and leave entitlements for parents and children.

There may also be extra supports and entitlements if, for example, your child has special needs.

The facts below were correct at the time of going to print but may change in the future.

GP visit card for children under 6

Children under the age of six are entitled to free visits so they can go to see a GP who participates in the scheme. All children under six who live and intend to live in Ireland for one year are eligible. This card also covers out-of-hours and urgent care. The GP visit card also covers your child for assessments at ages two and five and provides care for children with asthma up to the age of 6.

Many GPs take part in this scheme. To see if your GP does, go to hse.ie and search for 'under 6s GP visit card'.

If your child has a medical card

If your child already has a medical card, you don't need to register them for the GP visit card.

However, if your family circumstances change and your family is no longer eligible for medical cards, you can then register your child for a GP visit card if they are under the age of six.

Registering for a GP visit card

You will need to register your child for the card. This can be online or by post. See hse.ie for details. If you have any questions before registering, you can phone lo-call 1890 252 919.

Health service schemes

There are schemes to make the cost of medical and healthcare more affordable.

Examples include:

- medical cards
- the Drugs Payment Scheme
- European Health Insurance Cards (EHIC)
- GP visit cards

Some schemes are means-tested. A means test examines all your sources of income. However, some income is not taken into account when your means are calculated. See citizensinformation.ie for more information on means-testing.

Other schemes are based on age groups. Some are available to all residents.

See hse.ie for more information on these schemes.

Adoptive benefit

Adoptive benefit is a payment to an adopting mother or to a single adoptive father from the date your child is placed with you. Both employed and self-employed people can claim it.

For more information, contact:

- Social Welfare Services on lo-call 1890 690 690 or see welfare.ie
- Citizens Information at your local centre, phone 0761 07 4000 or see citizensinformation.ie
- your employer

Paternity leave

You are entitled to two weeks of paternity leave following the birth or adoption of a child if you are the:

- father of the child
- spouse, civil partner or partner living with the mother of the child
- parent of a donor-conceived child
- spouse, civil partner or partner living with the adopting mother or adopting father of the child

You can take paternity leave at any time in the 26 weeks following the birth or adoption. You must tell your employer in writing at least four weeks before you start your leave.

Paternity benefit

Your employer does not have to pay you for paternity leave. You may be eligible for paternity benefit for this time off.

For more information, talk to your employer or contact Citizens Information at your local centre, phone 0761 07 4000 or see citizensinformation.ie

Child benefit

Child benefit was previously known as children's allowance.

It is paid to the parents or guardians of children under 16 years of age, or under 18 years of age if the child:

- is in full-time education
- is doing Youthreach training
- has a disability

Who to contact

- Citizens Information – contact your local centre, phone 0761 07 4000 or see citizensinformation.ie
- Social Welfare Services (child benefit section) – lo-call 1890 400 400 or see welfare.ie and mywelfare.ie

One-parent family benefit

One-parent family payment (OFP) is a payment for men and women under 66 who are bringing children up without the support of a partner.

To get this payment you must meet certain conditions and do a means test. You can get more information from your local Social Welfare Office. Lo-call 1890 500 000 or see welfare.ie

Other benefits you may qualify for include:

- Back to work allowance
- Back to education allowance
- Disability payment
- Domiciliary care allowance
- Exceptional needs payment
- Working family payment
- Medical card
- Rent supplement
- Housing assistance payment
- Unemployment payments
- Back to school clothing and footwear allowance
- Health and safety benefit

Health or medical expenses

You may also be entitled to tax relief on health or medical expenses. See revenue.ie for information.

More information

- Citizens Information – contact your local centre, phone 0761 07 4000 or see citizensinformation.ie
- Your local Social Welfare Office – lo-call 1890 66 22 44 or see welfare.ie and mywelfare.ie

The information in this chapter was correct at the time of going to print but may change.

Finally

We wish you well with your family. This is such a special time for you and your family. You are supporting your child to grow up to be healthy, resilient and confident.

Look after yourself

Be kind to yourself, it is important to mind yourself and your relationships.

Don't be afraid to ask questions

Trust your instincts and don't be afraid to ask questions. There is no such thing as a silly question.

There is no training for having your first child and you are learning as your child grows about what works for you and your family.

More information

This book is the final part of a series of three books. Go to mychild.ie for more information on your child's health and development, plus advice on parenting.

Enjoy this time

Enjoy your child, have fun and create lots of family memories. Give your child the skills to solve problems, to plan ahead, to become confident and independent as they grow and develop.

Learn to take care of yourself too and prioritise this special time for you and your family.

Index

Index

Notes

You can find more tips and advice about pregnancy, babies and young children at **mychild.ie**

Notes

Notes

You can find more tips and advice about pregnancy, babies and young children at **mychild.ie**